Living In Love

LIVING IN LOVE
Connecting To The
Power Of Love Within

Christine A. Adams

Health Communications, Inc.
Deerfield Beach, Florida

Portions from *A Course in Miracles* ©1975, Reprinted by Permission of the Foundation for Inner Peace, Inc., P.O. Box 1104, Glen Ellen, California 95442. *A Course in Miracles* may be purchased from the Foundation for Inner Peace. The three volume hard cover set is $40. The single volume (all in one) soft cover is $25. The hard cover (all in one) is $30.

The ideas presented herein are the personal interpretation and understanding of the author, and are not endorsed by the copyright holder of *A Course in Miracles*.

Library of Congress Cataloging-in-Publication Data

Adams, Christine A.
    Living in love / Christine A. Adams.
        p.   cm.
    ISBN 1-55874-278-6
    1. Recovering addicts — Religious life. 2. Co-dependents — Religious life. 3. Twelve-step programs — Religious aspects. 4. Course in miracles. 5. Spiritual life. I. Title.
BL625.9.R43A43   1993   93-24748
291.4'4—dc20   CIP

©1993 Christine A. Adams
ISBN 1-55874-278-6

Publisher: Health Communications, Inc.
             3201 S.W. 15th Street
             Deerfield Beach, Florida 33442-8190

Cover design by Andrea Perrine Brower

This book is dedicated
to
EDWARD SHERIDAN HANLEY
1934 – 1992

*A courageous, caring man
who saw everyone as
a child of God, who
understood that
giving and receiving
are one, who used
his energy to co-create
love and who knew
the power of defenselessness
combined with compassion.*

*A father who taught his children,
and me, much about life
simply by living in love!*

Contents

Acknowledgements

My thanks to Barbara Nichols, editorial director at Health Communications, for her dedication to excellence, her encouraging words, and her wisdom as she lovingly guided this book to publication. And to Homer Pyle for his excellent copy editing.

Edward and Michelle Hanley, my son and daughter-in law, for their example of fortitude, faith and friendship.

Marcia and Michael Firsick, my daughter and son-in-law, for their love, laughter and loyalty.

Mark D. Hanley, my son, for his honesty, courage and constant caring ways.

Robert J. Butch who gently touches my being with his love as we "hold each other sacred" in each day and event of our lives.

John F. McKenna, my brother, for his steadfast, unrelenting strength.

David and Linda Shaheen for the generous sharing of their home and their hearts.

To all those who have touched my life with love!

Christine A. Adams

Introduction

Most of my childhood and early adulthood were spent dealing with loss. I did not think about spiritual progress because I was preoccupied with surviving. Through the years alcoholism had disrupted my life and the life of my family, creating dysfunction that left me ill-equipped to deal with my future. When I was fourteen years old, my father died leaving my mother with eight children from ages two to fourteen. I was devastated.

After attending a Catholic college, where religion rather than spirituality was taught, I began my search for self in accomplishments, money and marriage. Alcoholism destroyed my marriage as it had plagued my family of origin. It nearly killed me. Alcoholism cheated our children of family unity and left them to cope with problems peculiar to adult children of alcoholics. Finally I left that marriage and admitted that I could no longer drink in safety.

At forty years of age I joined a 12-Step program that changed my life by promoting a physical, mental and spiritual recovery. Physically I withdrew from alcohol and all mind-altering substances each day, one day at a time. I attended 12-Step meetings and associated with other recovering alcoholics who could help me in my recovery. The obsession with alcohol left me. The losses stopped and, for the first time in my life, I began to move forward to gain new physical health, new clarity of mind and a new feeling of self-worth. This was just the end of the beginning.

Getting Honest With Myself

In the first year I found myself alone bringing up three teenagers. It was a fight for survival and I felt frightened, desperate and ashamed. Nevertheless I had surrendered to God, knowing I couldn't go it alone any longer. There was no place for me to go so I turned to the people in the 12-Step programs and asked for help. They told me to pray, to practice the 12 Steps and to hang on. I did as they said. At the end of that year, I got a sponsor and did a Fourth Step inventory of my life which I shared with my sponsor.

The next two years were spent dealing with the knowledge gained by that Fourth Step inventory. With the encouragement of my sponsor I began to get honest with myself and admit to my most glaring defects of character. Slowly I did as Step 6 advises and asked God to remove these defects. My mind began to clear. During these years I went back to school taking 43 credit hours in alcohol- and drug-counseling courses. This knowledge became the basis for my writing and a foundation for my sobriety. I had settled my account with the disease of alcoholism by staying sober and learning about it. There was no doubt in my mind about the deadly, insidious power of addiction after these studies. If my own denial ever allowed me to minimize the significance of my own disease, my course work reminded me that addiction kills and that if I ever lose sight of the power of addiction it will kill me. It took learning, coupled with my own experience and that of others, to free me mentally from any reservations about addiction. I knew I could never use alcohol and other drugs safely. I had taught English composition and combined my professional expertise with my knowledge of addiction to begin a writing career.

Other Dependencies

In the fourth year of my recovery I began a co-dependent relationship in which my partner became my addiction. Although I felt the need for a committed relationship, I did not know that adult children of alcoholics have issues that need to be attended to before they enter into commitment. I began to attend ACoA meetings just as I entered this brief second marriage. When I discovered I had married a man with an active sexual addiction — a need to have affairs with other women — I realized our marriage was inoperative and left. My first book on adult children of alcoholics was published shortly after this unhealthy relationship ended.

Darkness To Light

Years six and seven were dark and desperate times for me as I discovered how devastating co-dependency is. I began my spiritual recovery at this point. My decision to file for divorce precipitated a time of turmoil and confusion. But out of this struggle came the beginning of my recovery from co-dependency.

I learned that co-dependency is a spiritual issue that stems from a lack of spiritual wholeness. I began to experience more honesty, more growth, more understanding about other dependencies that destroy lives. I began to write about sexual addiction and co-addiction.

In the eighth and ninth years I was faced with surviving the loss of a marriage and the terrible shame and social censure that co-addiction had brought into my life. It left me shaken. I had to look carefully at myself and at all of my relationships. Patiently I read, learned and wrote about co-dependency. My second major book was published at this time.

Some unusual circumstances within my marriage led me back to organized religion. A small ray of light came through as I practiced my religion and found solace. For the first time, religious practices offered me spiritual growth. A new spiritual awareness developed and began to break through the darkness.

More Light

In years ten and eleven of my recovery, I started attending meetings to study *A Course In Miracles* at my church. It is a self-taught course in spiritual transformation. Because these meetings were held immediately before the Sunday morning service, they were easy to fit into my schedule. Even though I still attended 12-Step meetings during the week, I thought *A Course In Miracles* might give me an added spiritual dimension. I had no idea the three volumes of the course would so profoundly change my perspective, move me to peace and commit me to love. At first I just considered it a part of my church program. Then it became much more. By helping me to get out of the victim role of the recently divorced co-dependent, it showed me that forgiveness was a gift to me. It personalized my conscious contact with God and gave me the spiritual strength and support I needed to live. As I began to learn the *Course*, I found myself unable to record my experience in writing. In those early years the ideas just washed over me and cleansed me.

Spiritual Changes

In the thirteeneth and fourteenth years of recovery, new spiritual awareness grew through my continued study of *A Course In Miracles*. The first and most profound change came when I accepted the teaching, "I am a child of God." After that idea became internalized I began to discover how to live as a child of God. My behavior gradually changed as I was released from old ego-centered, co-dependent patterns. I embraced discipline and saw it as a vehicle for joy in my life. Prayer became sacred and coveted, God was closer now and I was no longer afraid. Others noticed changes in me and wondered where I got my sense of peace. They asked me what it meant to be a child of God. They asked me how to get peace of mind. Slowly, I began to record disjointed phrases and ideas but it did not yet evolve into a pattern.

Glorious New Beginnings

Finally I no longer felt the need to people-please. I started being totally honest, telling the real truth, setting boundaries and living freely as myself. The first signs of healthy relationships began to emerge as I became present for them. It became okay to be alone, to be in or out of an intimate relationship with a man. It meant loving all people, not just special people. My view of my surroundings, my actions and my reactions changed. This change in perspective has left me open to people in my life and, more importantly, open to God. Out of these perceptions came the framework for *Living In Love*. It is only a beginning for me, but I know it is the most glorious beginning of my life. It is my hope that my words and experiences assist you with new beginnings as you move forward in your own spiritual recovery.

You Are A Child Of God

1

No matter where you are in life, no matter what is happening, you are always doing the best you can do with the knowledge and awareness you have. You are perfect just the way you are. There is no timetable and you can't progress too slowly or too quickly. You are perfect in your imperfection. You are always a child of God.

Do you sometimes think you are not enough? Do you tell yourself that you are not smart enough? Not attractive enough? Not good enough? If you have the vague sense of not being "enough," you are not alone.

Many psychological difficulties — anxiety, underachievement in school, emotional immaturity, sexual dysfunction, chronic spells of depression — can be attributed to low self-esteem. Many people suffer from insecurity, self-doubt and guilt, and are afraid to participate fully in life.

In his book, *How To Raise Your Self-Esteem*, Nathaniel Branden says, "How we feel about ourselves crucially affects virtually every aspect of our existence . . . as our responses to events are shaped by who and what we think we are." Branden continues, "The tragedy is that so many people look for self-confidence and self-respect everywhere except within themselves and so they fail in their search." He goes on to describe positive self-esteem as a kind of "spiritual attainment."

Usually thinking you are not enough is a spiritual issue. It disavows the existence of the spiritual self and indicates you are relying on human powers alone, not the power and presence of God. Thinking you are not enough indicates a lack of faith and a misunderstanding of your true nature as a child of God.

One of the reasons for not accepting our spiritual selves might be own lack of forgiveness. In our human frailty, we all err. Yet, if we can't get beyond our mistakes, we may never see our spiritual selves — that is, the forgiven child of God. Self-esteem is the reputation we acquire with ourselves. When we remember only our mistakes, see only our frailties and picture ourselves as sinful, we cannot find that child of God within.

It is in our internalized conviction as children of God

that we finally see that we are enough; in fact we are holy, chosen ones. It is in our connection with God, with love itself, that we learn to love ourselves and live in the power and glory of God's love. It is true that we are never enough in ourselves, but in the light of our inheritance as God's children and in the light of God's Love, we are everything, we are whole, we are perfect and we are enough.

If I could say only one thing to you, I would say, "You are a child of God." Then again and again, "You are a child of God." For me, coming to believe that I am a child of God was the most important transformation of my life. It meant a re-imaging of self. Once this was accomplished a change in self-esteem quickly followed.

But how does one become a child of God? By becoming willing to change and let God make the transformation. By letting Him into our lives.

When I started the 12-Step program, I kept hearing the words of the Third Step, "Came to believe that a Power greater than ourselves could restore us to sanity." For me, finding that Power meant returning to childhood, getting in touch with my inner child and then getting in touch with my Creator.

The first thing I did was to search for a picture of myself as a child. When I found it and positioned it on the shelf, I realized that if God is in me now, He was also there within that child. What a healing realization. Truly I was not just a child of this world, not solely of my parents, but a child of God.

This single experience enabled me to begin learning about my inner child, to reach back and remember her as she really was. It was at this point that I started letting God in to heal her within me. My task became to attend to that child's needs, to change the negative messages given to her, and to re-image that child into God's child.

Sometimes I was easily led back to an image of myself as "less than." I returned to seeking perfection, needing love while feeling unlovable, seeking control while feeling out of control and looking for security in an unsafe world. Often I returned to the old patterns, feeling feelings I thought I was not supposed to feel, seeking acceptance and not knowing I am acceptable, desiring maturity but remaining that child. The transformation began when I first acknowledged, without blaming my parents, the neglect that child had known. Then I nurtured that child, and, finally, changed my perspective. Ultimately, I knew that, in reality, I am in God and with God — God's child.

It was a matter of finding the perspective of faith — the coming to believe. God did not make us to abandon us. He did not intend us to view ourselves and our environment with distrust. God made us to be His children and promised us His unconditional love and care. This thought emerges again and again in *A Course In Miracles:*

> *I am sustained by the Love of God.*
> *As I listen to God's voice, I am sustained by His Love.*
> *As I open my eyes, His Love lights up the world for me*
> *to see. As I forgive, His Love reminds me that His Son*
> *is sinless. And as I look upon the world with the vision*
> *He has given me, I remember that I am His Son.*

The essence of the *Course's* teachings is the concept that the Divine breaks through from love itself into each life. Thus each person represents a spark of the Divine and is interconnected with all creation. That perception of each of us as a child of God helps us to see our mission in life clearly and to let go of the fear that destroys the love we generate from within.

With my change in perception came a change in the negative messages that had controlled me since childhood. In my recovery from alcoholism, there was a spiritual awakening. My shame was replaced with respect, and the new child was prompted to emerge. In recovery, I learned that God is the one who can sustain the positive messages

I need to hear. This reversal from the negative to positive helped me to re-image myself as a child of God. Then when *A Course In Miracles* reiterated those ideas, I was ready to hear.

My journal entry at that time more clearly details the process:

> I've become aware of the power of God within me. It is the growing consciousness, and I need to keep in contact with that power. His power can put me above selfish pettiness; it can move me in directions I would not dare move otherwise. His power can sustain me through the pain of any loss.
>
> I've come to believe that the most important ingredient in my life is the power of God within. It will be my sustaining force until I return to Him. Those who love me will not sustain me, nor will the material possessions that make me comfortable make me whole. Only that power of love within me that I call God can sustain me without fail.
>
> Through the years I've tried to experience my own sense of power in other persons, in position and in things — and that would sustain me for a while. Eventually, though, that connection would dim. I then returned again and again to the spirit within where I found the power of God. That power never dims.
>
> Today, when I am troubled by others who would harm me, I think of this power of God within me, and I know I am loved. If I try to protect myself from all harm, I will be ineffective. But if I let God protect and guide me, I know I'll be cared for. God is a safe new place.

When we look outside ourselves for our identity we are bound to fail. The world is far too transient. When we look inside, claiming our rightful spiritual identity as a child of God, we are bound to see our true selves.

Low self-esteem is a spiritual issue. It is bound up with our inability to see that which is within us, our inability to connect with the perfection within our imperfect human body, to connect with our souls.

"I Am Lovable"

The first negative message that changed for me was "I am not lovable." If I am of God, of Love itself, then that meant "I am lovable." God loves me unconditionally.

When I re-imaged myself as a child of God, I emerged as a less needy, more loving person. No longer did I depend solely on others for affection, attention and love. I depended on God. My happiness in a relationship was no longer the responsibility of my partner. What a burden! What an unrealistic expectation! I was no longer controlled by others, led out of myself and torn away from my own center of peace and serenity. Unhealthy co-dependence had always led me away from God because I believed that in and of myself I was not lovable. It would take my partner's love to make me lovable, not my self-love to keep me whole.

Other very important issues were brought to light with this new perspective. If I am of Love itself, then I have the right to be treated in a loving way and the responsibility to maintain self-love and discipline. No longer could I allow abuse in my life. No longer could I live without the dignity due a child of God. So I set limits in relationships, communicated my needs in a loving way, no longer feared abandonment and refused to accept physical or psychological abuse.

When I accept myself as God's child, I see myself as loved and loving, as perfect in my imperfection. There is joy in that recognition. Great joy.

When The Student Is Ready, The Teacher Comes

Whenever I need a teacher, God puts one in my life. This time it came through my classroom in the form of one of my students, a lovely young woman named Rebecca.

On the first day of class the students seemed edgy and concerned. It became clear they were angry about Rebecca, who was not present for the class.

"I don't care, I'm glad we told," Melinda whispered.

"Are you sure she won't be in big trouble?" another asked.

"She is already in big trouble!" Melinda quickly interjected.

It was clear that this class was not going to function until Rebecca got there. The door opened and an attractive blond hurriedly entered the room, taking her place in the circle. A tense silence gripped the room.

"They are trying to tell me what to do," she said aloud. No one dared to speak. As if in mockery of the seriousness in the room, the chorus next door started to sing. Rebecca took that as a signal to begin as she shuffled in her chair and opened her book. Everyone watched her and did the same.

Rather than going on with this tense, distracted class, I decided to challenge Rebecca.

"Who is trying to do this, Rebecca?" I asked.

"They think I jumped in front of Bill's car intentionally last night," she answered. For the first time, I noted the scratches on her face and arms.

"My parents want to put me away," she said disgustedly. "It's that Student Assistance Team — they think I'm crazy," she went on. The rest of the class reacted with concern and sympathy. Rebecca was their friend.

Very quickly I realized that as a teacher I was in risky territory and tried to defuse the situation by saying that each case is individual and that the team might not be right in every case.

"I don't know your situation, Rebecca," I added.

With that the class slowly moved to begin the lesson. The next day the principal called me into his office.

"I got a call from Rebecca Howard's parents last night and they were furious," he said a bit agitated.

"What happened?"

"Did you tell Rebecca that the Student Assistance Team was wrong in her case?"

"Never," I said emphatically, realizing that Rebecca had taken what I said out of context. The moment I realized how desperate and how clever Rebecca had been, I became angry.

The principal explained further that Rebecca used what I said out of context in the emergency meeting at the psychiatrist's office at a local hospital yesterday afternoon. She was building her case so that she might not be hospitalized for her self-inflicted wounds. She was determined to stay with her boyfriend whom she was obsessively attached to.

I had to face her the next day. At first I felt used and betrayed, but eventually I recognized that her desperate actions sprang from a sad and lonely place inside. I decided not to confront her but to help her and be there for her.

When I got to know Rebecca, I recognized that she was suffering from co-dependency in its most severe form. She really believed that if Bill left her, she would die. Bill was charming, captivating and controlling, and in her mind she thought she did not have enough of herself to make it without him.

It was a long, dangerous year for me and for Rebecca. With each crisis, I listened. Having just ended a destructive co-dependent situation in my own life, I could relate. Rebecca became my teacher. She became an example of the dangers of thinking you are not enough, of believing that someone else holds your life in their hands. I talked her through many days when she did not see how she could go on.

"You are a fine writer, Rebecca, the best in the class," I told her. She heard only partially because her mind was always on Bill. Then slowly she began to gain strength. I think she knew that I had suffered through co-dependency and was making my way out of it. We leaned on each other for a year until she graduated. She and Bill may still be together but Rebecca is a stronger person today. She no longer chooses to harm herself when he retracts his love because she has developed her own sense of worth. God always sends me a teacher when I am the most in need. Rebecca was one of the best.

"I Am Safe"

The second negative message that changed for me was, "I am not safe." If I am of God, of love itself, then, "I am safe!" At all times the love of God will keep me safe and guide me. Even though I continue to see tragedy and sickness around me, the world has become spiritually safe for me because God is my parent, my protector.

I have learned to listen to my inner self in order to discern what might be dangerous. When I sense danger I look to God for the courage to proceed. Bad things do not elude me but my perspective has changed.

I first initiated trust in my life by developing trust in God. Then it spilled over into relationships with others. Over and over again, I turned my life and will over to the care of God as I understood Him; and, over and over again, He did not fail me.

As long as I remember "God's will for me is joy," I can accept seemingly unfortunate situations. Many times I did not know the results of some loss until long after it had occurred, but I knew that God would never abandon me and that in time I would see some good from a seemingly bad situation.

Just this week I was reminded of this truth again. Jennifer Hodges, the daughter of a close friend of mine, was

killed in a helicopter crash. Jennifer was the nurse on the
Life Star helicopter that rescues accident victims and car-
ries them to Hartford Hospital, Connecticut.

Ironically, she was killed trying to rescue someone. Her
death shocked and moved thousands of people. On the
night of the wake, I stood in line for four hours with
thousands of others outside the funeral home. It started
to rain. The hundreds of emergency medical technicians,
firefighters and policemen in line took out plastic garbage
bags. They handed them back through the line and we
covered our heads. Lightning flashes cut the sky and the
rain poured down, yet no one went home. We all stayed in
line, inching our way into the funeral home. Five thousand
of us!

When I finally reached Jennifer's father, a deeply spiritual
man, he hugged me and said the most remarkable thing.

"Some good will come out of this. You will see, Chris.
You will see."

I could not think of one good thing at the time.

The next day the memorial and burial service was held
at a large city church that could seat only a fraction of the
thousands who wanted to get in. A sound system carried
the words of tribute from Jennifer's coworkers to the
crowd. Parents whose children had been saved by Jennifer
and Life Star wept on the lawn, children whose parents
had been saved wept as well.

When Jennifer's cremated body was placed in the earth,
the Life Star helicopter passed over the church. There
wasn't a dry eye in the crowd.

Some might see no logic in Jennifer's death. She was so
young and dedicated, so vital in her work, helping to save
this man's daughter, that man's son. How could I really
agree with her father and see anything good in her death?
At that moment, it seemed difficult.

On reflection, however, I realized there was great ho-
liness in the outpouring of love at the time of Jennifer's

death. Those thousands of people who work to help others were united in one place at one time to honor someone who believed in love and lived in love.

Never could I have re-created a more profound example of living in love than what I saw at Jennifer's funeral. At the interment, the Life Star helicopter passed over the gravesite as a reminder that her loving service will continue.

At that moment, it was clear that Jennifer's death had great meaning. She did not die uselessly. Her love went on in the renewed dedication of every service person there. Her love continued on in each mission of that helicopter and in each loving act of her colleagues.

Love is like that — it does not end with the giver. Love flows on to the next person and the next and the next. Love brings more love.

"I Am Okay"

The third negative message that changed for me was "I am not okay." As a child of God, this message no longer fit. It became "I am okay."

As a child I felt unacceptable, and I would invariably try harder, striving for perfection in all areas of my life. If I were perfect, I had a chance of forging order out of the disorder in my life. Ultimately, it became clear to me that perfectionism didn't work. It was only through my connection with God that I could be okay. When I understood that I am God's child, not God, I could accept my limitations and failings.

Accepting our true selves creates a paradox by asking us to forgive ourselves our human frailties on the one hand and to view ourselves as perfect spiritual beings on the other. Only when we see through this seeming contradiction, and rid ourselves of trying to be perfect, can we come to love ourselves.

When we can come to understand ourselves as perfect spiritual beings, or children of God, we are ready to love

ourselves as God loves us. It would be hard to conceive of
the energy of God as a conditional force, one that picks
and chooses its subjects to love. Therefore, we are asked
to forgive ourselves our imperfections and love ourselves
unconditionally. Is that easy? Not always. But it's ever so
necessary for peaceful, positive and powerful living.

Louise L. Hay writes in *The Power Is Within You*, "We
usually make loving ourselves conditional, and then when
we are involved in relationships, we make loving the other
person conditional also."

So it is that we find it difficult to love another until we
love ourselves. Here are some simple rules for loving
yourself:

1. *Be gentle with yourself*

Everything takes time. Therefore, give yourself the time
you need to love yourself. When you forgive yourself, you
lift a great weight off your shoulders. All of us are at
exactly the place we need to be at any given moment. Give
yourself permission to grow and to come to the awareness
of life. What is your hurry? Be kind, but not indulgent. Be
kind to yourself. You are God's child.

2. *Be kind to your mind*

Fill your mind with positive affirmations. You are worth
it. Don't abuse your precious mind with negative thoughts
and digressions. Say nice things to yourself every day.
Begin with the words, "I am God's precious child." Be kind
to your mind by praying, meditating, reading positive
words and visualizing positive outcomes.

3. *Stop criticizing yourself*

Loving ourselves means that we don't beat ourselves up
by telling ourselves that we are bad or dumb or worthless.
Stop mercilessly judging yourself. There is nothing wrong
with you. You are God's child.

4. *Stop scaring yourself*

Sometimes we carry around a sense of impending
doom. Let it go! You do not need to be afraid. Fears of

abandonment and rejection are not real, so stop scaring yourself. There is nothing to fear when you rely on the love and power of God.

5. *Praise yourself*

Don't listen to your own negative defamations. Give them up in favor of positive affirmations of praise. Tell yourself, "I am wonderful." Not just once, but all the time. You are a wonderful child of God. Praise your strengths and accomplishments. If you can do it for even one minute at a time, it will help. Talk to yourself as a loving God would talk to His child.

6. *Accept all things as good and be grateful*

So often we see only the negative side in an event or happening. Look for the positive side. Ask yourself, "What is the lesson which I must learn?" Look for it and be grateful.

Life's paradoxes often weave intricate patterns of forgiveness for us. I once found myself needing to forgive myself for betraying a trusted friend. That mistake stayed with me and I never fully forgave myself.

Then a trusted friend betrayed me in exactly the same way I had betrayed my friend. I was filled with a hatred and rage, which I thought I'd never release.

After a long, desperate struggle with anger and grief, I realized this woman had been my teacher. She had given me a precious gift. She became the vehicle for me to give forgiveness and, ultimately, to experience God's forgiveness for myself. I knew that if I could forgive her, I could see myself as washed clean of the harm I had once done to my friend.

I knew I'd found a special key in that experience. Now when I think of the woman who harmed me, I smile. Through her betrayal I attained a great personal victory.

"I Am In Control"

The fourth negative message transformed in me was, "I am not in control," which became, "I am in control." Until this realization took hold I had wavered back and forth between trying to exert unreasonable control over people, places and things and abdicating, giving up control completely. My behavior was oppressive, disruptive and confusing.

Finally I realized the only thing that I could reasonably control was myself. All other attempts were futile and frustrating. For the truth is, no matter what we fear, no matter what is at stake, we are not in control of much in life except our happiness, our personal behavior, the way we treat and think about ourselves and others. That is enough. All else is in God's hands.

As God's children, we will not be abandoned even when things seem impossibly out of control. In times of crisis, we need to consciously turn our lives, and the circumstances of our lives, over to God. We are responsible only for ourselves.

If my children drink abusively, it is not my responsibility; they are in control of their own actions. If my husband is unfaithful, it is not my responsibility; he is in control of his own actions. If I am subject to someone's jealousy or anger, it is not my responsibility; I am not in control of others' feelings. If someone is irresponsible, it is not my responsibility; others are responsible for their own irresponsibility. If someone is intolerant of me, it is not my responsibility; they are in control of their own attitudes.

All we can possibly control in any situation is our own thinking and behavior, the choices we make. If we listen to internal negative messages and choose negative behaviors, we could meet infidelity with infidelity or drunkenness with drunkenness or anger with anger. We could be intolerant or irresponsible.

Or we can take care of ourselves and guard our own
actions in the sight of God. We can decide to live in love.
Others have to be responsible for their relationships with
themselves and God, just as I am responsible for my relationship with myself and God. God knows what is best
for others as he knows what is best for me. If I allow Him
to be God, I won't deem it necessary, or even desirable, to
control others.

With this in mind, we can erase any negative message
from childhood that says, "I am not in control," and replace
it with, "I am in control." Tending to ourselves and to our
relationship with God ultimately allows us to experience
ourselves as being fully in control.

"I Will Always Be Helped And Protected"

The fifth negative message to be changed was, "I will
not be helped and protected," which became, "I will always
be helped and protected."

If we experience ourselves as children of God, we know
we are not alone. We will be helped. All we need do is ask
— and have faith that our answers will come. God can
and will steer us toward the proper decisions. In His love,
he can and will show us what steps to take. He can and
will help us to maintain our self-respect, dignity and
values. There are no broken promises or lies with God,
just truth and love. We can rest assured that all answers
lie within us if we just ask for help to see them.

A Course In Miracles repeats this idea many times and in
many ways:

> God is my strength. Vision is His gift. You will see
> because it is the Will of God.

As we know the help and protection of God, there will
be an integration of self, a "making whole" and a sense of
spiritual well-being that comes over us. Because we have

changed our perspective we no longer see ourselves as fearful. We are safe.

In the final stage of my re-imaging of my self, the negative message, "I have little faith," became, "I have great faith in God and God is the love in which I live."

During this process, I was moved to a greater sense of my true self, to my true spiritual depth. My spiritual life, my union with God as His child, is personal. I have discovered faith in my own way and time just as you are finding it now.

My faith has become useful in my day-to-day life, providing basic ingredients for living: trust, freedom and joy. It's experiential, like 12-Step work and *A Course In Miracles*.

Though words cannot explain fully the meaning of being a child of God, it is possible to accept the truth of it in the center of your being. You can break out of all your old images of yourself and into a new, more spiritual self. One of love itself.

The old message, "I have little faith in God," becomes "I have great faith in God." Gradually you realize that your faith in God is not only your greatest treasure, it is all you need.

Living As A Child Of God

2

Living out the role of a child of God is not an easy task but it is the only one. First, we need to make conscious contact with a Higher Power and maintain that contact. Next, we need to know that this personal relationship with a loving God is our primary relationship.

How do you live as a child of God? By turning your life and your will over to His care and reminding yourself that He is in charge.

When I accepted the concept that I am a child of God, my life began to change. I came out of the darkness into the light of love. Out of the darkness of insecurity, oppressiveness, obsessiveness, co-dependent living and fear. What a dark spot that was! I can clearly remember those feelings of impending doom that stalked me like some relentless predator. But when I intentionally changed inside, my life changed on the outside, too.

As I said in the last chapter, we need to assimilate the powerful positive messages of *A Course In Miracles:* "You are a child of God." "You are perfect, just the way you are!" "God loves you the way you are and I love you the way you are!" Start with that knowledge and go on from there.

Gerald G. Jampolsky, a pioneer in presenting the concepts of the *Course,* has been one of my teachers. In his work *Out Of The Darkness Into The Light: A Journey Of Inner Healing,* he clearly details his transformation after reading *A Course In Miracles.* There was a time for Jampolsky when he realized that he had been listening to the voice of his ego — a voice of fear that told him he was "alone in a world of scarcity." He attempted to rely on his own intellect, will, judgment and past experience but ended up feeling empty and isolated. Love was always conditional in those days.

Jampolsky says:

> Through my study of *A Course In Miracles* I began to realize that there are only two ways to make decisions: The first one was already familiar to me, the old way of listening to the ego, the voice of fear and separation. The second was one I just began to learn, which was to listen to the voice of God, a voice based on love and joining.

21

So it was with me. My spiritual path was marked by this struggle to live in love, to come out of the darkness into the light of God's Love. I was encouraged by my teachers, and the new, lighter feelings that my personal work of transformation was beginning to engender, to accept my role as a child of God and accept and love others as His children. With this oneness came peace, with this oneness came courage and hope. In Hugh Prather's work, *There Is A Place Where You Are Not Alone, Reflections On A Course In Miracles*, he says:

> What we know we know because we are one. In our oneness is perfect knowledge and peace, but in our conflict, controversy and specialness, there can be only despair. Even though they may choose to hear it at different times, God speaks to His children all at once.

Believing that there was a scarcity of love only made me conserve it. There could never be enough! Believing that defensive attack thoughts could protect me, I set up barriers, looking for a security I didn't need. In truth, I was terrified of my own impending doom, ultimately my death, my final separation. It seems the very autonomy I sought was destroying me. Finally I was forced to give up — to surrender!

Marianne Williamson in *A Return To Love*, says:

> Surrender is not weakness or loss. It is a powerful non-resistance. Through openness and receptivity on the part of the human consciousness, spirit is allowed to infuse our lives, to give meaning and direction.

It took surrender for me to find peace, joy and even glory. I had to lose in order to win. When I established my true identity as a spiritual being, I understood my real purpose in life. When I realized I am of love itself, I heard not only the voice of my ego, but of love as well.

In preparing to write this book, there were times when my ego said: "No one will listen to this message. Who are you to pretend to have something to say about love, about God?" Then I came to know we all have the same message of love in us and we all need to hear it and express it. For that reason, I can say I love you because we are one — and I do!

Until I read *A Course In Miracles*, the voice of my ego told me, "I am unprotected, unlovable, alone in a frightening world. Nothing can save me. Every time I do anything, I do the wrong thing. I am not okay. There is no point in trusting anyone or anything because people, places and things will harm me. Be careful — take care of myself. Who do I think I am, anyway? Why do I think I am so great? I am so stupid! I am no good."

With this monologue going on in my head, it was no wonder I felt a sense of impending doom. It was as if I were defeated before the battle had begun.

The voice of my ego told me that if I looked carefully, I could find one special love relationship that would bring me happiness. It told me to think of myself and my family first, and to get as many material things as I could. It told me to demand and get my way, to manipulate and control people. It helped me measure people by what they had and what they could do for me.

My ego told me I'd better remember the past so I would not be hurt in the future. It made me hate failure and helped me make idols of certain people. It helped me to people-please, be unforgiving, blame others, live as a victim and be exclusive in my relationships.

The voice of God does not speak in these terms. Jampolsky tells the wonderful story of how he made the decision to treat his patients without charging fees. It was a daring move. Then his first book, *Love Is Letting Go Of Fear*, became a runaway bestseller and his financial problems were solved.

I do not suggest you follow his example unless you feel so directed. However, I do believe that much of society's directives are generated by the ego-voice rather than the voice of love. We dehumanize the homeless, minorities and the poor so that we will not have to empathize with them. If we truly lived in love, we would help them. There is much to do and a long way to go.

We may not all make drastic changes in our living circumstances as Jampolsky did, but we can experience change through surrender and learn to live in love. Marianne Williamson says:

> Something amazing happens when we surrender and just love. We melt into another world, a realm of power already within us. The world changes when we change. The world softens when we soften. The world loves when we choose to love the world.

A Course In Miracles explains that the voice of the ego always tells us there will be disaster, but without the ego there would be love. It is this love that is the business of the child of God.

Once I have internalized the concept of being a child of God, I can go on to change old behaviors. I can ask two important questions: Is this decision a loving one? Is this action self-destructive, self-effacing or self-indulgent? A child of God lives differently from a child of the material world; yet, I live in and of this world.

Instinctively, we all know we need to return to that loving place inside.

Sometimes in the morning when I anticipate an unusually trying day, I read this in *A Course In Miracles:*

My only function is the one God gave me.

Whenever my ego-thought system returns, all things are conditional. I measure, get, plan and calculate. However, when I am living in love, I forgive, extend and teach love through the power of a defenseless state. I am giving myself to others freely — just because it is natural. From this loving place I can live a better life and make more ethical decisions. There are many practical ways that this theory can be demonstrated.

One of the simplest concepts is this: If I am a child of God, I will not allow myself to be treated in a disrespectful way. Never! When this does happen, I will note it and confront the situation, if appropriate. Then I will quietly and lovingly go on with the realization that the persons trying to harm me are not aware of their own loving nature. I am who I am and that never changes. Their attempt to harm me is a "cry for love." I need only respond lovingly and refuse to accept the abuse. My peace of mind will remain intact.

As a child of God I also reject self-abuse. I will not knowingly harm myself. How could I try to destroy one of God's children? How could I devalue what God values? Never!

When I started my recovery from addiction, I studied alcohol and drug counseling and met two male teachers. One seemed reserved and cool while the other seemed loving. One loved with discipline and restraint; the other loved to satisfy his own need to be loved, to quell his own fear that he was unlovable.

The first was a minister and a teacher. Although he probably didn't know it, he taught me some very important lessons about life. In a three-week seminar at his home in Maine, he taught about alcohol and drug addiction. He and his wife worked together to run the summer program. She cooked, cleaned and played the piano — and loved him. He taught, encouraged his students — and loved her. Every day he would run five or six miles at dawn. In the afternoon he chopped the wood, and in the evening he helped his wife in the kitchen.

I was just getting sober, feeling desperately alone and needing attention and love. Physically, this man was extremely attractive to me; emotionally, I would have related to anyone. Quickly and quietly, he set his boundaries with his students and we respected those boundaries. It remained that way through several years of course work.

The other teacher, equally attractive, set no boundaries. I felt uncomfortable with him in our first meeting. It was his voice, his manner, his unexpected intimacy that bothered me. As I watched him over the next three years, I noticed how many women became inappropriately attached to him and spent too much time speaking with him, becoming improperly tied to him emotionally. His inappropriate expressions of concern and affection put me off, but I didn't know why. Later, when I learned the difference between conditional love and unconditonal love, it became clear. Love to him meant conditions — the constant attention of women.

Real love does not harm others, take from them or leave them broken and afraid.

Sexual addiction runs rampant in our society, leaving many people broken and afraid. That kind of love is not living in love, even though the sex addict seems to love everyone. That's just the problem! Sexual addictions are caused by psycho-spiritual issues that stem from the need to draw from someone else's love when we can't love ourselves. When we have not internalized our role as a child of God, when we do not know we are of love itself, we are apt to try to convince others to love us. If it works, what better proof of our lovability than this conquest? This behavior is not love but soul sickness. My first teacher was operating out of a place of spiritual strength; the other, more popular one, out of spiritual weakness.

Whenever a self-defeating thought comes to my mind, there is a voice that says, "I am God's child." It is difficult to rationalize self-destructive behaviors, such as consuming mind-altering drugs or living co-dependently, when your mind is saying, "You are a child of God." It is difficult to engage in any negative behaviors when your inner child is saying, "I love you, my God," and the answer comes, "I love you, too, my child." How much more nourishing these words are than the self-destructive messages of the ego.

So it is with living as a child of God. We start by cleaning our own house, clearing out the dishonesty, intolerance and lack of discipline in our lives.

The 12 Steps are successful because they emphasize recovery through the cultivation of ethical values and inner guidance. After the first three steps, where we admit we are powerless over alcohol (or other substances), admit our lives are unmanageable, come to believe in a Higher Power and turn our lives over to that Power, we begin to examine our behavior. The Fourth Step calls for a searching moral inventory, which we share with another person in Step 5. Then in Steps 6 and 7 we are asked to have God remove all defects of character, and in Steps 8 and 9 we make a list of those we have harmed and make amends to them when we can. Step 10 tells us to continue to take a personal inventory and admit when we are wrong. Step 11 brings us into contact with God again and Step 12 asks us to carry the message of hope. These 12 Steps are the practical formula for living a life guided by ethical values.

The 12 Steps are simple, yet they are difficult to live. They lead us away from resentment, away from self-loathing to self-love and forgiveness. By making amends, we can turn loose the unhealthy guilt which has kept us mired in self-pity. We learn to handle situations that normally would baffle us.

We become decisive and worthwhile human beings by rigorously following the 12 Steps. We then have a chance to live as children of God.

There is little room for depression, guilt, boredom, fear, loneliness or anxiety if the 12 Steps are followed. They work! Transformation doesn't happen immediately be-

cause the 12 Steps imply stages of progress, the beginning
of an entirely new way of living.

Does this sound like work? You bet it is! Relentless, joy-
producing work.

With vigilance and patience, millions of recovering persons use the 12 Steps as a workable way to maintain a
spiritual life. Step 11, which suggests a program of
prayer and meditation, acts as the fuel to keep the other
steps going.

Step 11 reads:

> Sought through prayer and meditation to improve our
> conscious contact with God *as we understood Him*, praying
> only for that knowledge of His will for us and the power
> to carry that out.

The first word of Step 11, "sought," suggests action.
When I seek, I am actively looking. Prayer is not a passive
endeavor. I associate peacefulness with prayer because
praying may bring peace of mind but praying itself implies
a conscious effort on my part to contact God. Therefore,
in order to have a prayer life, I need to develop a program
of prayer. Having a regular program of prayer implies
that I think of prayer and meditation as a normal part of
everyday life.

Somehow I couldn't really accept prayer as a regular
part of my life until I began to reap the benefits of it.
Practicing the Eleventh Step made me feel better, think
better and live better. That's a difficult combination to
turn away from. Once I set my program for prayer in
motion, it began to carry me.

Somehow when I start my day right, it stays right. As
a recovering alcoholic with 14 years of sobriety, I always
start my day with a simple request — that God might
keep me away from one drink for one day. Then I go on
to the daily meditation book of my choice. I've used different books over the years because I have changed in my

spiritual growth. There are many ways to choose to start the day.

By starting my day with a meditation from *A Course In Miracles*, I can go back to that thought as the day progresses.

There is no particular time for prayer and meditation. If you "seek" to pray, you find time during the day to make conscious contact with God. Any moment can become a prayerful moment. Here are some kinds of daily prayers:

1. *Prayers of Praise*

There are what I like to call holy moments all day long. During those moments we can thank God for His beneficence. It can be as simple as seeing a child, having your car start or being able to successfully finish an important task. Whenever two people share a loving moment, that is prayer. Whenever someone forgives, that is prayer. Whenever anyone makes a decision to stay away from a harmful situation, that is prayer. Whenever people meet and share their experience, strength and hope, that is prayer.

Prayers of praise are the fillers of my day as I observe all the things in my life I wish to thank God for. They come in a flash of appreciative contact with God.

2. *Prayers of Petition*

There are many people and situations in our lives that are beyond our control. Asking God to deal with them is a prayer of petition. Whether it is a critically sick friend or a bothersome neighbor, I ask God to do what I cannot. I can do simple, helpful things and then I must turn those people and situations over to the care of God.

There is little use in being overcome by fear, anger or resentment. The best I can do is release it and pray that God will take care of that person or situation. Prayers of petition can free us from people and situations over which we have no control.

3. *Prayers of Acceptance*

In the Eleventh Step, we "pray only for the knowledge

of His will." I believe that frequent prayers of praise and petition during the day help us to learn the knowledge of God's will. When we look at the world with praise and gratitude, we are more likely to see the many gifts God gives us. When we see these gifts, we accept the good in our life. I believe God's will for me is joy. I need only see it. Acceptance always brings joy.

When we are able "to turn our will and our lives over to the care of God as we understood Him," we begin to accept some of the things we do not yet understand. Prayers for acceptance are closely tied to my petitions for God's help with people, places and things in my life — because by admitting I am powerless over those things I accept that God is in control. I succumb to His plan even when I don't understand the outcome. I simply believe, without fear, that "all things work together for good for those who love God."

4. Prayers for Power

There is no greater power than God. I must turn to Him whenever I need the power to go on with my life. Faith dispels fear and prayer increases faith. So whenever there is the overwhelming presence of fear, prayers for power will help.

No matter what the day brings there is an unending source of power for us to draw on through prayer. All I need to do is connect and reconnect with God's power throughout the day. During the day I remind myself with these prayerful affirmations:

- God is with me. I live and move in Him.

- Peace to my mind. Let all thoughts be still.

- This day I choose to spend in perfect peace.

- God is the love in which I live.

Ending the day in prayer has special meaning. It can be a time of inventory when we ask God to help us see what might have gone wrong during the day. It can be the moment we ask for forgiveness and resolve to make amends or the moment we thank God for another day.

Evening prayer doesn't necessarily need to be structured as you kneel beside your bed. It can just be a heart-to-heart talk with God before you sleep. Prayer is a wonderful way to end a day.

By lifting my heart to God in daily prayer, hope, peace and joy are restored to me. That is my daily grace, my personal miracle.

The Importance Of Putting God First

Living as a child of God implies a workable relationship with God. It means involvement and communication. In all relationships, I expend certain energies to be successful. So it is with God. If I am to reap the benefits of a personal relationship with God, I need to place my relationship with God before all human relationships.

But what about one's wife, husband or children? How can anyone come before them? God is our primary source of love, peace, power and glory. Through our spiritual connection with God, we reach out to the spirit of those we love. It is really all one love, but so often we forget, *"God is the love in which we live."*

Recently I heard a member of a group say that he had always felt a certain "spiritual disquietude" that could only be filled with his relationship with the Divine. For him, nothing else could fill the emptiness inside. I knew exactly what he meant!

My feeling of emptiness didn't mean that God ever left me but that I chose to move away from God. Other relationships became primary — my husband, my children, other family members. I lost track of the fact that "God is the love in which I live." First and foremost, it is God and me. All other relationships fall into place when I recognize this truth. If I am to bring strength and courage and hope to anyone else, where will I get it? By making contact with God and by relating to others in a loving way.

Making a human relationship primary and neglecting God causes me to lose my way.

If you find yourself co-dependently relying too much on a spouse or child for inner meaning, it might be good to re-evaluate your relationship priorities. It will help to re-structure your relationships by giving more time to God.

When anything is important to you, you devote yourself to it. Your relationship with God is the most essential thing in your life. If you don't attend to it, you won't reap the benefits of the union. The inner spiritual void will remain.

People often say they need more time to work around the house, to relax, to play, to be with friends or family. How often do people say they need time to pray or get reconnected with God? A spiritual relationship is personal and requires reflective, quiet times. It doesn't just happen; we have to set aside the time.

Sometimes when I need to get back to God, I go back to Maine where I was born. Across from the house where I grew up there is a suspension bridge that spans a portion of the York River as it makes its way out to sea. The river flows into the harbor here and sometimes it holds more beauty than I can bear. I went there when my father died, then my brother, my mother, my child and my husband. Each time the flow of water energized my soul and the beauty of a sunset brought peace.

Sometimes by the ocean in Maine, I find a flat rock high above the other rocks and sit in the sun. It is the calm of the rock that is so familiar, the grey-white slate colors that dry as the day goes on. Barnacles, snails and seaweed, ugly and beautiful at once, lie at my feet while crabs crawl around the sea floor to keep me company. Paths by the ocean are overgrown with red and white sea roses — a quiet place of gentle beauty that reminds me of God's power and permanence.

It is in these quiet places that I recognize my part in God's universe is simply to accept whatever changes come to me, to go on without holding onto the pattern of yesterday and to see what beauty is in this day. In these places of my childhood I turn to God like a child, giving Him control of my life, letting Him guide me. Once again I recognize my prayerful connection with God as my most important relationship. Once again I feel loved, protected and cared for at all times. In these places I come home to love itself.

Forgiveness

3

Forgiveness is our primary function. It is a gift to ourselves. If we forgive ourselves, we will begin to trust ourselves. When we say we don't trust life or others, we really don't trust ourselves. Trust helps us to see all others as children of God and to offer them the gift of forgiveness — just as God offers it to us.

In keeping with *A Course In Miracles*, I have made forgiveness my primary function. Forgiveness is the way to peace of mind. Why hold back? Some people believe forgiveness is a gift to those who have harmed them. It isn't. Forgiveness is always a gift to ourselves. Holding back forgiveness simply means we are unable to forgive ourselves. Release of another person through forgiveness is release of self.

When I hold back forgiveness, I am into my own ego, dealing with illusions of what *should have been* or judgments of *what others should have done*. My last book, *Love, Infidelity And Sexual Addiction* came out of the experience of co-dependency and sexual addiction. It presented the co-dependent's view of being married to a partner with the disease of sexual addiction. One of the principal chapters in that book was about forgiveness.

Without *A Course In Miracles*, I could not have internalized the concept of forgiveness as a primary function in my life. I had to understand that there was no other choice for me if I were to gain freedom. I had to come to understand that true forgiveness would benefit me. Through genuine forgiveness of myself and my partner, I came to know real peace.

After all, addicts and co-addicts are involved in the same "wrong." If you are sexually addicted and love "too many," and I am co-dependent and love you too much, what is the difference? Both dysfunctional behaviors are the same. Both partners are looking outside of themselves for self-worth. Both partners are trying to fill a spiritual void. *A Course In Miracles* says:

> **Those who forgive are releasing themselves from the illusion, while those who withhold forgiveness are binding themselves to illusion.**

The illusion is that we are separate entities, not children of God sharing a common salvation. The illusion is that if we forgive, we will be condoning someone else's sins. The illusion tells us that if we declare someone else sinless in the eyes of God, we will be less. They might be right and we might be wrong. The reality is that we are all one, all perfect in the sight of God. It is our primary function to forgive, to change our perception and see others as God's children.

When I withheld forgiveness, I had a need to deny my part in the problem and to stay in my sickness, my separateness, my illusion. Releasing my husband after his repeated infidelities was my first step to freedom and peace of mind.

A Course In Miracles speaks of the "holy instant": "a time in which you receive and give perfect communication." There are many holy instants in our lives. Moments that are somehow touched by the Holy Spirit — moments of intense healing. We can appreciate those moments as we forgive, as we search for healing.

Jenny crossed the Piccard Bridge as the onslaught of four o'clock traffic broke loose. It was hot and her silk dress clung to her back. Her temples were wet — a single rivulet of sweat made its way down her neck.

Perhaps I should have said six o'clock, she thought. Then we could have avoided the traffic. Screeching brakes startled her as she closed in on the car in front of her.

"Never mind, I know this is right," she said aloud. "This is what I have to do!"

She was nervous. She admitted it. It had been two months since she had seen Paul, and she heard he was going to remarry his first wife next month. Bitter thoughts of betrayal and hurt crowded in as an angry motorist honked at her. Paul didn't give me much leeway, she thought. They will be remarried ten days after our divorce. Again, anger and resentment welled up in her.

"It is not for me to judge. I am accountable for my thoughts and actions," she said. Somehow her spoken reassurances helped her to go on.

Yesterday, when Jenny called Paul's office to ask for this meeting, there was hostility in his voice, but he agreed to meet at the restaurant. Now she wondered if he would burst into anger again. Or would she become silent and unable to speak? As she neared the restaurant, she wondered if she could sit down with a man who had been her husband, betrayed her and would soon remarry his first wife.

"I'm not sure of what I am doing," she muttered as she turned into the parking lot. She saw his car. With a deep breath she straightened her jacket, another deep breath and she entered the restaurant, praying that she could do what she had come to do. Smiling, she walked to the back of the restaurant where Paul was waiting.

For a few minutes she said nothing. Neither did he. She continued to smile. Suddenly there was calm within her. No hurry — just peace.

"I am happy to be sharing the space with you."

"What?" he asked. Her loving comment caught him off guard and he looked like he might cry. It was an awkward moment.

"I am happy to be here with you," she said, still smiling. "I just mean that it feels good to be sharing the same space with you." More silence.

Finally, he said, "You look good!"

"I am good," she said. No response.

A waitress asked if she wanted coffee. Jenny nodded and the woman filled her cup.

"More coffee?" she asked Paul.

"It's always over coffee, isn't it?" Paul said. "Some things never change." They both laughed.

Jenny began to address the issue at hand. She spoke of her part in their marriage, reiterating where she felt she had gone wrong. Not once did she refer to what he had done.

Tears came to his eyes. He had not expected this. Her defenselessness was overpowering.

"But I was wrong," he said "I am the one to ask for forgiveness. I need to ask you to forgive me!"

"No, you don't," Jenny said. "It is already done! The reconciliation between you and me has already taken place in the mind and heart of God. All we need to do is catch up, to recognize what already is."

After a long silence, he nodded and smiled again.

She returned the smile and repeated, "I am happy to be able to share this space with you today!"

"Yes! I am too," he answered.

The space of forgiveness they shared that day was special, even sacred. It is like that with forgiveness. There is power in defenselessness. It leaves an everlasting mark. It is the primary function in all our human relationships.

Letting Go

Gerald Jampolsky puts it this way:

> Forgiveness is the vehicle used for correcting our misconceptions and for helping us to let go of fear. Simply stated, to forgive is to let go.

By letting go, we surrender and turn to God for the answers. When we realize we are powerless, we are able to look to God for help. Then God becomes the solution. Thoughts of God replace obsessive thoughts, and we gain release from all that has robbed us of freedom.

Any obsession is an attempt to fill a spiritual void. It is an inner gnawing that never gets better, no matter what you do. It always returns to plague you because that spiritual void can only be filled with love. And that love will extend to others in forgiveness, our primary function.

In the daily lessons of *A Course In Miracles*, we read:

Forgiveness is the only gift I give.

At first it takes enormous concentration and courage to let go of obsessions. Trying to control anything except my own spiritual growth is futile. Simply put, it means "Tend to your own business." And the business of a child of God is love. Love is what you are, love is what you do. Love does not resent, hate or attack — it forgives. Forgiveness is the function of love. In order for me to be true to what I am, I must make a decision to forgive myself first, and then others. Love forgives all. There is no picking and choosing, even when we feel gravely wronged.

When forgiveness becomes my primary function, I begin to accept the challenges of life in a loving way. There is no spiritual separation in this stance. If I am a child of God, forgiven of all errors, so are you.

All of us are joined to God through His love. Love does not judge or exclude. Therefore, we are asked not to judge or exclude. That does not mean I have to agree with everyone's ideas and behavior or accept abuse. But I must forgive. In order to be free, I must let others go.

To forgive, it is not necessary to forget. If I have been the victim of someone else's behavior, I must remember it to prevent it from happening again and to avoid victimizing others. If we forget, we may repeat that situation again with different players in a different scene.

We can condemn someone's behavior while respecting the sanctity of the individual. It is not our job to absolve anyone of the harm they may have inflicted on us or those we love. Absolving is an act of judgment and a positioning of the ego. Absolving says, "I am better; you are worse."

Forgiveness says, "I love you." Forgiveness is not self-sacrifice or a pretense of being good. Once again, that

positioning comes from ego-based thinking that puts me
above you. Forgiveness is a gift to the one who forgives.
It is a decision to enter a process of healing. It is a decision
to let go of anger, resentment, ego, self-pity and personal
hurt. It may take time but it is a gift to the self worth
waiting for.

You might say I can't forgive this person or that one
particular incident. It seems impossible to let it go.

But to have peace we must be willing to let the wound
heal. If a sore is left to fester, it will get worse or it will
get better in a random way; but if a wound is tended to,
it should heal. So it is with any damage inflicted on us.

By choosing to hang on to old hurts, we remain victims.
People may feel sorry for us and we may not have to be
as responsible as we could be. After all, we have undergone great trauma. Why shouldn't we be given a little
leeway? There is an illusion of being the "good guy" when
you are the victim. God loves us all. There are no "good
guys" or "bad guys," just forgiven children of God. This
is the time to actively drop the victim role and embrace
healing — it is a time to forgive.

How To Let Go Of Resentment

To hang on to resentment is to harbor a thief in the
heart. By the minute and the hour, resentment steals joy
we could treasure now and remember forever. It pilfers
our energy to celebrate life — to face others as messengers of grace rather than ambassadors of doom. We
victimize ourselves when we withhold forgiveness.

Think of it this way — think of your soul with a dark
negative spot in it — a sick place that keeps out the light
of your being, a dark place that never gets healed. Why
wouldn't you let it go? Love gets rid of resentment, anger
and malignant hatred that infects our souls. Forgiveness
gives light. It heals and brings peace.

I say this only metaphorically, as I do not believe my spirit is marred with dark spots. These dark spots represent a lack of vision coming from my own ego. When I believe I have been wronged, and carry a resentment toward another person, I am blind to the real truth.

In a spiritual sense, darkness is malignancy, a lack of light, a lack of energy. *A Course In Miracles* has taught me that my spiritual being is of God's love. It is unchangeable, a resource of energy never failing. It is my ego which obscures it.

By staying in my ego, I can remain "right" in all situations of my life. Life becomes a battle to prove that I am better than you, that I am right. You are 100 percent wrong in any given situation and I will prove it. That kind of thinking keeps all hurts alive. It is useless to reenact the creation of the wound. We all feel we have been injured, and healing those wounds is more important than rehashing the circumstances of the hurt. If I could like my life without hurting others, I would be more than human. Much harm is done inadvertently by all of us.

By looking at forgiveness as a weakness rather than a strength, we think we are showing an adversary that he can't get away with hurting us. In reality, we are keeping the wound open and unhealed. An unhealed wound poisons us. Life is not a matter of personal power over others. It is more a matter of connecting with the power within us. Forgiveness is a gift to me.

Through illusions, I convince myself that everything would be perfect "if only" this or that had not happened. Life happens — good and bad. Expecting to get through it without any scars is not realistic. Perhaps when I say, "If only he or she hadn't done this, I could be happy," I am really saying I choose not to heal that wound; I choose not to let go and go on. Perhaps I am not willing to summon the courage to process the hurt. Perhaps I am making excuses for my inability to live in love. Forgiving implies hard work; it involves process.

Watch a physical wound heal. It changes day by day, needing different treatments at different stages of recovery. So it is with forgiveness. Any healing process will take different forms depending on the nature of the hurt and the depth of the wound. Here are some stages of spiritual recovery you might encounter. They might not appear exactly in this order, as each person processes differently. There are times when you might backtrack and become reinfected with the sickness that brought on the hurt.

1. Denial

In this early stage, we tend to deny the intensity of the hurt and play down our feelings about the situation. However, the hurt is there and it will resurface to get our attention.

2. Self-Blame

There is a tendency to be judgmental. How could I have been so stupid as to trust that person? Why did I accept a situation at face value? Sometimes in hindsight we think we see how things might have been different if only we knew then what we know now.

3. Victim

We tend to wallow in self-pity at this point and become less disciplined because we are sorry for ourselves.

4. Anger

Eventually anger sets in and we get mad at the person who hurt us or perhaps at the world or, even worse, at God. We become less tolerant and more self-righteous.

5. Self-Forgiveness

We begin to see that the situation taught us some valuable lessons which we might not have learned any other way. Perhaps a similar situation that we handle in a different way reminds us of what we have learned. Then we are grateful for the lesson. We survive and go on, knowing we did the best we could with the knowledge we had at the time.

6. Forgiveness Of Others

We acknowledge that people who hurt us did the best they could at that time. We recognize that although we do not accept or condone their actions, they are also children of God and need to be viewed as more than their negative behaviors. We can let go and release the energy we were using to blame them and ourselves. We can now become healthy, unencumbered and peaceful.

How To Heal Spiritual Wounds

Just as physical wounds heal in stages, so do spiritual and emotional wounds. When I contracted a severe case of poison ivy, my skin at first erupted in tiny pink blotches. Then the skin stretched to make white blisters, and as the poison got into the bloodstream, these blisters became blood blisters. The infected area had a scarlet hue and became unbearably itchy. Finally, after constant treatment with cold packs to dry the skin and doses of steroids, the infection began to subside. It was not an immediate cure. There was a process in recovery as well. The blood blisters became white again and scabbed over, turned pink and finally disappeared. At any stage of this process the sight was repulsive. However, the healing was assured by a constant and systematic attack on the poisoning.

So it is with the healing of a spiritual wound. Most spiritual injuries are not attractive. Take a woman in an Al-Anon meeting who has been beaten by her drunken husband the night before. She is so broken and immobilized with pain that she can barely function. Look at her a month later. Her face might still be tense and distorted with rage but the bruises are gone. Look at her later and the lines on her face might have hardened into resolve and strength. It may be years before you will see serenity in her expression and brightness in her eyes, but if she continues to heal, it will come. It will come if she is willing to heal through forgiveness.

The path of forgiveness is not a straight line, as the stages of healing are never linear. We slip and slide, back and forth, in and out of denial, anger and awareness. Be patient with yourself and be assured that if you work at it willingly, you will be healed. You are a child of God, perfect just the way you are today.

Forgiveness overlooks all hurts. It is possible to have a moment of moments, a miracle of immediate forgiveness. It is possible to instantly forgive as Christ did, but most of us in our humanness process the hurt until it heals.

A Course In Miracles taught me a new perspective and helped me to see in a different way. It helped me to see all people as *one* — forgiven in the sight of God. That new perspective helps speed the healing process:

Forgiveness offers everything I want.

A Course In Miracles asks, "What could you want that forgiveness cannot give?" What is there beyond peace? What is there beyond, "a sense of worth and beauty that transcends the world?"

There is nothing of this world that can be substituted for the peace of mind that forgiveness brings; therefore forgiveness becomes our primary goal.

The *Course* sees forgiveness as the ultimate basic redemptive tool. As Hugh Prather observes, we always look at something someone else has done, or what that person symbolizes to us, with annoyance or resentment, even if it is momentarily. This allows us to look inside ourselves and see a trait of our own that we have not yet been willing to forgive; another's resentment of this same trait in us is his greatest gift to us. We literally must bless our enemies because they are the trigger for our forgiveness of ourselves.

By not bringing any past hurts, any past perceptions or interpretations into the present, we reach a point of at-one-ment. This connects us to the limitless reservoir of love that permeates the universe. The *Course* says you can choose at any moment. Even one instance of forgiveness fully experienced and fully understood will allow transformation. Equally, any one resentment will preclude this transformation because it casts a dark shadow on the universe.

So long as we have one resentment, one unforgiving thought, the entire creation is incomplete.

Therefore, as long as we maintain the problem is not in us but in someone else, our attention will have been successfully diverted from the source of the problem. The ego tells us to go outside ourselves — blame others. To counter this pattern, we allow God to speak to us from within — where He is.

To teach only love, there must be a source of love available at all times. Here is where God within us really comes into focus. If we are of God, of love itself, then we must be loving too. It is here within. We need only find it. Each day I repeat these words adapted from the *Course:*

God is the Love in which I forgive myself.
God is the Love with which I love myself.
God is the Love in which I am blessed.
No fear is possible in the mind beloved of God.
God is the Love in which I forgive.

In the Eleventh Step, we find that through prayer and meditation we can reach inside ourselves to make conscious contact with God. From that contact, we are empowered to function with forgiveness, to preserve our own happiness and to teach love.

When mentally scattered and pulled apart by the things of the world, we can't become centered enough to deal with others. We lose our way sometimes. Prayer and meditation can return us to the source of our power, to God, to love itself.

The life that functions in forgiveness is balanced in prayer. Just as it says in Step 3 of the 12 Steps: "We made a decision to turn our will and our lives over to the care of God, as we understood Him." Just wanting to forgive, to strive to forgive, to pretend to forgive, won't work. Forgiveness has to come from the center of the spiritual self. It has to come from the knowledge that God is a forgiving God whose children abide in His constant love. Seeing ourselves as children of God helps us to see others in that light — the light of forgiveness. Forgiveness is a profound metaphysical happening. First, we accept forgiveness from a loving God; then we extend that forgiveness to others. This process is not easy to understand because it is of God's love — a miracle.

Albert Camus describes the death/rebirth experience in this way: "In the midst of winter, I finally learned that there was in me an invincible summer." We go to our invincible summer when we reach inside to pray.

When we truly surrender to a loving God, accepting His forgiveness for us as well as others, we are at peace, we are healed. To withhold forgiveness is to be less than what we really are — children of God. When we hold back, stay in the past, wish to be right or remain a victim, we do not really wish to be free. Perhaps we have not yet established a clear picture of ourselves as children of God, filled with love and joined with our brother. Perhaps we do not really believe as Christ taught that God's plan for us is to be joined in love. Forgiveness is the starting place — the only place to grow spiritually.

The Power Within

4

The more we connect to the power within us, the more freedom we have. When we turn our life and will over to the care of God as we understand Him, we can feel free to live one day at a time. There is a sense of acceptance within us, a noticeable absence of fear, a peace that quiets us.

The power within me comes from the realization that I am a child of God; however, this realization did not come easily. It meant giving up other roles to embrace this new one.

I am *first* a child of God, and second the child of my worldly parents. It is undeniable that I came from my parents and that they shaped me. I accept that parenting. Yet in a spiritual sense I am a child of God. My parents were also children of God — living and acting in an imperfect world with their own set of difficulties. We are all God's children.

My ability to see the shortcomings of my parents and still deeply love them is contingent upon my ability to see myself, and them, as children of God. In addition, my own children's ability to see me and themselves as children of God has made my human errors bearable to them.

For me, the realization and internalization of that one truth — "I am a child of God" — has empowered me.

Marianne Williamson in *A Return To Love* addresses the reader with these words:

> You are a child of God. You were created in a blinding flash of creativity, a primal thought when God extended Himself in love. Everything you've added on since is useless.

There is a source of energy within everyone who accepts that connection to God.

I believe *"Love which created me is what I am."* Therefore, I need not seek anymore because love prevails and that is what I am.

With the realization of the power within comes a new freedom. The things of this world — the pain, the indecision, the inequity, the loss — all seem less formidable. Whenever I had to handle these things alone, I felt overwhelmed, but now it is easier. There is a new freedom — not exactly an absence of fear but an understanding of it.

Reading *A Course In Miracles* has given me a new perspective. The world hasn't changed as there are still disappointments and disasters, but my view of the world has changed. That is my new freedom. No longer does the outside world dominate my spiritual inside world. For me, this new perspective is a miracle.

Being fearful was a state of my own ego — my human condition. Alone I could do nothing, but connected to God I gained power. Fear can be diffused with the power of God's love — the power within.

Living with an understanding of fear and dispelling it through faith helps me to live more fully. Not immobilized all the time, not hesitant, not overcome with anxiety, but free.

A state of freedom generates its own peace. I do not feel as "fear driven" when I am conscious of my true self — that is, my connection to God. It is cyclical, for faith brings power, freedom and peace as fear dissolves in my mind.

The lessons of *A Course In Miracles* speak of this peace:

Now will I seek and find the peace of God.

How To Lose Yourself
To Find Yourself

For years I battled life with the idea that alone I could conquer anything. It was my duty to solve all my problems by myself, to search for answers and act on decisions by myself. God was there but not as a part of me. Today I sense a power within, a spiritual part of me, of love itself, that drives me when my human power fails. In the past I resorted to other escapes for relief from my fear. Today I need no escape, just the realization that I am a child of God and that I am never alone!

It would be senseless to believe that God could abandon his children; therefore, if I believe I am His child, it follows I will never be left alone and unassisted.

There is great comfort in the realization of being parented by God. With it is the assurance of comfort and company at all times.

Perhaps the most frightening thought for any of us is the thought of death. Being a child of God means knowing that God will not abandon you in any moment — but particularly that last moment.

So living life and even leaving it becomes more manageable when we walk with God, knowing a loving father or mother would never abandon their own child. It is just a matter of awareness, perspective and the knowledge that this spiritual power is ever available to us if we are willing to reach out to it.

Alone I am powerless over world situations, over certain substances that might imprison me, over addiction and addictive situations and over others whom I might wish to control. But with God's assistance, and only with God's assistance, I can regain power. By having to admit how powerless I am, I have been driven to a more spiritually powered life — to my real role as a child of God.

When I surrendered to my addiction, I was desperate, with few or no resources left. Here is where faith came in. Powerless, I had no place to go but to a Higher Power. Since no human power was effective against my addiction, God became my only source of strength, my only hope.

I remember experiencing a sense of terror when I finally knew that I could not go on drinking. There was no place to go. What I had denied so long became the truth — "I am an alcoholic," I thought. "God help me." And He did.

Addiction was like having a huge leech attached to my body, draining my blood. I had tried to remove it many times and failed. I was terrified at being powerless to stop something that was destroying me. I knew it would take some powerful outside force to pull the leech from my body. I found that the outside force could only be God. Finally, I surrendered and asked God to remove it.

It seems ironic that losing control to alcohol or drugs, or becoming addictively involved in a relationship, can be the guide to a more spiritual place, but it was for me and millions of others who are involved in 12-Step programs. When addiction shows up in our lives, we are forced to surrender or die — we recognize how frail we are without the help of God.

In *A Return To Love*, Marianne Williamson says:

> People are crashing into walls today — socially, biologically, psychologically and emotionally. But it isn't bad news. In a way, it's good. Until your knees finally hit the floor, you're just playing at life, and on some level you're scared because you know you're just playing. The moment you surrender is not when life is over. It's when it begins.

God's help is always available. All we need to do is ask. Trying to control uncontrollable situations without the help of God usually leads to frustration and sometimes disaster. Through the 12-Step programs I got help by learning to turn my life and will over to God as I understood Him.

For me, turning my life and will over to God means acceptance of life on life's terms. It means understanding and accepting the unpredictable vagaries of life. It means giving up control of the uncontrollable.

When I am directing the show or playing God, I am not turning my will and life over to Him. Instead, I am thinking that I will not be happy until my child is free from this problem or that, until I am in the perfect union with the perfect mate or until I get a promotion, or even a job. Postponing my happiness "until" causes it to elude me. I can't always control events, but I can control how I react to events.

Preferences

Turning over my life and will to God means giving up addictive demands of God. It means accepting something that seems unfair. It means believing that all things do work together for good. There is a vast difference between demanding that life be a certain way and having a preference in a certain situation.

Ken Keyes, Jr., makes this point in *How To Make Your Life Work,* when he says:

> You automatically trigger feelings of unhappiness when the people and situations around you *do not fit your expectations.* In other words, *expectations create your unhappiness.* It's the *emotion backed demands* that make you suffer — it's not the world, the people around you or even you yourself.

Keyes says we need to work on changing these emotion backed demands to *preferences* and not let our happiness be controlled by our demands of life. In that way, happiness or joy are always an option and we can choose to be happy today.

Once when I was co-dependently caught up in someone else's addiction, I did not see the difference between demanding and stating a preference. My life was being overturned by my husband's sexual addiction. It was frightening and I was constantly threatened by the shame of his compulsive behaviors. With his repeated infidelities, there was the threat of social censure as well as the loss of the relationship itself, which was the most frightening of all.

Addiction destroys everything in its path. If you are involved with any kind of addiction — one who drinks too much, eats too much, wants sex too much or works too much — you will be feeling the losses that accompany addiction. It is inevitable.

As I reacted to my husband's addiction, my demands became stronger and stronger. He felt that I was trying to control him when I was really trying to control the addiction and the loss and pain. These addictive demands on my part were alternately resented and ignored by him. As a matter of fact, they helped him blame me and "stay in his addiction." The only way out of this trap was to stop trying to control and let go to God. This situation was beyond my control.

The only thing in this situation that I could control was *me*. My behavior, my attitude and my demands! Needless to say, I would have preferred not to be dealing with such a situation but there it was. I could cope with it by assuming no responsibility for his behavior or I could try to force my will on him.

At that time I could not discern what was mine to control and what was God's. In confusion, I left the marriage to avoid the terrible pain.

Today I accept this loss as part of a greater plan and understand that God's will for me is joy. Acceptance and forgiveness have brought that joy to me. Understanding has taught me about health in a relationship.

Since I prefer to be in a healthy relationship, I do all in my power to keep all my relationships as honest and as open as possible. I do not demand anything of anyone. And strangely enough, some wonderful moments of joy come my way — miracles, perhaps?

How To Give Up
White Knuckle Control

Being free means giving up. Giving up our will, our wants to God. Accepting life on life's terms, not our own, being willing to see that "all things work together for good for those who love God." Being free means admitting that we are not in control; we don't always get what we want but what we need.

No longer is it necessary for me to control all things — my will and life belong to God simply because He is more capable of handling them. Left to my own devices, I often court disaster.

Once again, the divine paradox happens. As we let go to God, we gain an immeasurable freedom of self.

However, freedom always implies discipline. At first I would balk at the thought of a stringent, even ethical interference in my spirituality. It sounded too much like sin and hell and damnation. Yet in time I learned that proper constraints bring freedom.

Embracing the disciplined life offers me options and opportunities. When I lead a good life I am at peace within. There is freedom — from secrets, self-reproach and self-anger. Whenever I hurt myself or anyone else, the peace of mind and freedom are gone. Therefore, I see life as a series of responsibilities that are peace producing, not grudging responsibilities, but ones that are embraced. How can I knowingly be involved in a self-defeating situation and feel at peace? It is impossible.

When I hurt myself in any way, I lose my peace of mind. Sometimes, the confusing part is in the seeming good in a hurtful situation. For example, drugs and alcohol relieve the pain of living for a short time. It seems good at the time, but eventually you lose.

So it is with addictive relationships. They are sometimes engaging, exciting and dangerous. However, it takes a sense of responsibility and discipline to turn dysfunction to function, sickness to health or to avoid these situations altogether. There is a responsibility to self — to that child within who deserves to be treated with respect and love. We cannot knowingly hurt ourselves and be at peace with ourselves at the same time.

We often hear in 12-Step meetings about "acting our way into good thinking." Psychologists like Lewis Andrews say there is a connection between spiritual values and emotional health. He says that psychotherapists are looking at the 12-Step programs which emphasize the

cultivation of ethical values and inner guidance. He says
there have been times when conventional psychoanalysis
and behavior modification have not been enough in the
treatment of alcoholism, drug addiction and other addictive behaviors.

In his work, *To Thine Own Self Be True*, Andrews, a
recovering alcoholic himself, says that depression, guilt,
boredom, indecision, feelings of worthlessness, fear, frustration, loneliness and prolonged anxiety have their roots
in particular judgmental and manipulative habits.

For example, depression could very well mask a "clini-
cal" resentment. Andrews claims that carrying a grudge
for a long time can produce a crippling mental condition.
Equally as debilitating is a "bout of guilt." Perhaps this
guilt can be traced to a situation where we need to rectify
the damage we've created, if possible. We really do need
to make up for what we do — to make amends and move
on. This kind of work takes discipline and direction.

To move beyond fear, perhaps we need to be honest
about our attachment to dangerous, fearful situations and
personalities. Did we become used to fears as a child? Is it
something we know? To live in peace we must choose social
interactions that are peaceful, that move on a spiritual path,
that provide personal growth — not places where the (fearful) action is. That takes direction and discipline.

To Be Free Inside, I Need To Act Right Outside
Or
To Feel Good Is To Act Good

The idea of discipline and freedom coming in the same
package is so simple a principle that it often escapes us.
There is no other prescription for peace — live the Ten
Commandments and feel gloriously alive with your own
sense of self.

A perfect child of God is free from secrets and hidden
agendas — no roles, manipulation, controls, co-dependen-

cy and resentments. A perfect child of God has no need
for self-reproach, self-anger and self-judgment.

When I see myself as God's perfect child living an honest life, I know I am doing the best I can do — for today.
When there is freedom and discipline in perfect balance, it
is easy to live one day at a time.

Each day I repeat to myself these words from *A Course
In Miracles:*

- **I am not weak, but strong.**
- **I am not helpless, but all powerful.**
- **I am not limited, but unlimited.**
- **I am not doubtful, but certain.**
- **I am not an illusion, but a reality.**
- **I cannot see in darkness, but in light.**

There is a direct correlation between acceptance and
peace in our lives. Whenever we truly accept the pattern
of our life as it is today, we are at peace.

There is always some good in any given situation. You
might not see it today, but it will show up later. Believing
— accepting — that God understands the plan better than
we do is faith. That's what living is all about, turning our
will and life over to the care of God, of love itself. That is
faith. That is acceptance, and acceptance brings peace.

When a loved one dies, it is hard to see the good in it.
Loss is never easy or desired. Last summer I had the
opportunity to spend two weeks with a friend who was
dying of cancer. My time was my last gift to him. It was
a rewarding experience because he accepted his death —
even at age 52. When John's life was solely dependent
upon machines, he met this challenge with dignity by
helping us with his mechanical know-how, patiently in-
structing us how to keep everything in working order.
Bodily functions were gone. He was castrated, had a bag
that held the elimination from his bowels and a computer-

fed dispenser of morphine hanging from his bedside. But he had great dignity.

It was the simple things. Like the greeting he gave the nurse or his genuine concern for a visitor's problems. When it came time to sign the documents that requested that he not be given any more fluids, it was John who signed. There was power in his acceptance, dignity in his death.

When we play victim, we give away our power. But when we take responsibility for our lives — through God we become powerful. Admitting we are powerless over other people, situations or substances makes us powerful. With the help of God, we can change our lives by admitting our powerlessness. Paradoxically, out of our admission of human weakness, we gain divine guidance and move on to greater things.

Using The Power Of God

5

The power of God, of love itself, sustains us if we choose to use it. We can connect with that knowledge and wisdom any time or we can refuse to rely on it. We can return to the past or we can make a conscious decision to let go, refusing to be a victim of the past any longer.

Connecting to the power of love within us is a choice. I can make that connection or refuse it. God will not move out of my path. However, I can choose to move away from God.

One of the ways that I refuse the power of love itself is to return to the past. Tormented and torn, I live only a partial life. I am besieged with second thoughts. "What if . . .?" What if I had done such and such, what if I had said this at that moment? What if . . .? These are "no-answer" questions, and if I continue to ask them I will have a powerless and unproductive life.

Living in the past is a conscious choice — a decision to remain a victim of circumstances. Whenever I play the victim role, I lose. God does not wish me to be a victim of life — rather God's will for me is joy.

The knowledge and wisdom of being a child of God gives me unlimited power, power that moves me from past failures to this moment in time. This moment is the only moment I can live today, but I must choose this moment.

When the past or future dominate my thoughts, I am in a powerless state. It takes all my energy to deal with life for one day. Yet it takes great wisdom to know how to stay in this one day. The Lord's Prayer says: "Give us *this* day our daily bread," and it is a wise person who looks to this day, one day at a time. *The Serenity Prayer* reiterates these ideas:

God grant me the serenity to accept the things I cannot change,
Courage to change the things I can,
And the wisdom to know the difference.

Living one day at a time,
Enjoying one moment at a time,
Accepting hardships as the pathway to peace,
Taking, as He did, this sinful world as it is,
Not as I would have it.

Trusting that He will make all things right
If I surrender to His will;
That I may be reasonably happy in this life
And supremely happy with Him forever.

Reinhold Niebuhr

The past is definitely one thing I can never change. Therefore, any hold it may have on me will rob me of the power I need to deal with the present. So it is with the uncertain future. Sometimes we get so apprehensive about the future that life today has no meaning. It is hard not to be apprehensive. But it is well to remember that the God who took care of you yesterday will be there tomorrow. Believing sometimes takes great courage. However, believing is a choice we can make. We can frantically cower in the face of the future or we can "expect a miracle." Perhaps the miracle of acceptance, patience or peace.

Connecting to the power of love within us — connecting to God — is a choice. We can choose to make that connection or refuse it.

Relinquishing The Victim Role

Another way in which we give away our power is to become engrossed in trying to control others by playing God. Ironically, when we admit we are powerless over people, places and things, we can regain our strength. We give back to God that which is His own and tend to our own inner strength, our own personal relationship with God.

Playing the role of victim is a good way to forget my inner connection with God. If I can say, "He did it to me" or "Life is unfair," or "The situation is hopeless," I can be sure of maintaining an unforgiving attitude, a lack of faith and a sense of despair. If I can blame others and society in general, I need not change my life.

Living in love starts with me. I am the most important person in the world. I am God's child and I can teach love to everyone I meet. Being God's child means not being a victim.

When I step out of the victim role, I become "the actor." Being responsible allows me to respond to a given situation rather than being forced into a response. Today I know I always have a choice and the power to change. *A Course In Miracles* tells me:

> **God is the mind with which I think. I have no thoughts I do not share with God.**

In *A Return To Love*, Marianne Williamson says:

> I never realized that depending on God meant depending on love. I had heard it said that God was love, but it never kicked in exactly what that meant.

If God is Love and we wish to follow Him, we have to learn to live in love, with love, by love, for love and then, and only then, will our minds be one with God. When we think with God, life is peaceful. When we think without Him, life is painful. We can choose to live in love each and every day.

Choosing Joy

By changing our perspective, we can be happy all the time. Yes, all the time. Asking God for help is always rewarding. He is never capricious and never punitive. God is love, and He will guide us even when we can't predict a joyful result. *A Course In Miracles* proposes that God, or Love Itself, dwells within us because we were created in His image, making us extensions of His love. If that is true, we are closest to our true nature when we are living in love. The Course proposes the relinquishment of a thought system based on fear, and the acceptance of a thought system based on love.

If we are living in love, we can find the answers to all questions and learn to listen to ourselves. Even when friends and family advise us, we can ask ourselves, "Is this a decision that is a loving one for me? Is it right for me now?"

God's will for me is joy. I have come to understand that I may not always like what is happening to me, but if I accept life on life's terms, I am joyful. Whenever I do not try to change a situation that can't be changed; whenever I do not hurt others or myself; whenever I do not insist on being right all the time, I feel joy. Whenever I accept loss and return loved ones to God in good condition, I feel joy.

Any changes that I make are going to have to come from within me. Just talking about change won't do it. Until I am willing to do both the mental and the physical work and ask God for help, nothing outside of me will change.

Whenever I am in the process of change, things tend to get worse before they get better. That is confusing for me. I panic and think "all is lost." It takes time to love yourself, believe in yourself and act accordingly.

Knowing what to do and doing it are two different steps. It takes time until I am strong enough in any new change — until I have made the complete shift. Until then I must be vigilant in my efforts to change.

Sometimes it is hard for me to accept that change requires action. I tell myself, "I am a child of God! I do deserve the very best!" If my actions do not prove that affirmation, I become confused. Being a child of God means living as a child of God.

It is with a measured discipline that I find joy. Having equated discipline with authority or drudgery, whichever seemed to fit at the time, I could not see the positive side of discipline. Now I know discipline can bring rewards.

It is through a disciplined life of prayer that I make a conscious contact with God. Only when I recognized this fact did I long for the discipline of regular times of prayer and meditation.

For me, prayer began to have an "indelible significance" or long-lasting effect, when I began to yearn for times of quiet prayer and reflection. It became elemental to my existence as I derived my inner peace from the words I read, and the meaning of those words returned to renew me during the day. It was this nurturing experience that made me wish to return to the peaceful centered state of prayer and meditation as often as I could. No longer was the idea of duty associated with prayer.

Similarly, it is through the discipline of asking for God's help that I achieve happiness in personal relationships. Happiness is peace of mind, living in love. To translate that into action is never easy. Using the power of God helps. It may mean leaving an addictive relationship to save both partners from certain conflict. Some loving actions seem to be unloving on the surface but are not. Being responsible for self and others in a loving way can cause loss and even pain.

Sometimes it seems easier just to give in to all the painful, difficult things in life and let them rule my life.

As a recovering alcoholic, I am constantly reminded of the discipline that holds my life together. It has been a matter of attending 12-Step meetings regularly, and being reminded to turn my will and my life over to the care of God. Without these meetings, I would be likely to return to the thinking that kept me in this addiction for years. With these meetings, I am reminded that a conscious contact with God can lead me to peace and joy.

I am constantly reminded that I need to stay out of co-dependency. It took an understanding of the spiritual sickness of co-dependent living for me to first pull myself away from living through others and begin to live for others.

When I am not living in a way that is loving for me or someone else, my gut reaction is so strong that I feel as if someone has just kicked me in the stomach. This almost overpowering feeling is my signal that something is terribly wrong and that I'd better get in touch with my Higher Power. Today I have the discipline to do that.

Today it is difficult for me to separate that discipline and joy. The unhappiness of my life comes in the form of dis-ease, or lack of peace, a churning within. Being aware of those warnings and doing something to correct the situations that bring them on are necessities for me.

If I find myself in any kind of unhealthy relationship, the warning bells go off! I can be drawn to these dramas and I know it. The change in me is not that I am never drawn into any unhealthy situation, but that I do not stay hooked. However, letting go is never easy. Ego and fear dominate unhealthy situations. If I do what is truly loving, peace and joy return to me.

When my heart is beating in the peace of God, I attend to His answers, not my own. It is there and only there that I feel at home. Surrounding me is all the life God created and I hear His call in every heartbeat, every breath. Here is peace and forgiveness.

Each heartbeat brings me peace; each breath infuses me with strength. I am a messenger of God.

I wonder about being the messenger speaking to others about God. Then I realize that I am only the messenger, and the words are already written. It is just my job to give them to the ones for whom they are intended. We are all messengers in every word we speak.

We are all messengers of some message. It can be one of fear or doubt, or one of love. Our gestures, the expression on our face, the intonation of our voice, all contribute to the message. Each life is a clear message. What does my life say? What does yours say? And what do we say together? These are important questions.

Sometimes it is difficult to ask ourselves these questions. No one is perfect. We all feel our lives could be better. It is not easy to see ourselves as clearly as we are perceived by others. The world judges by various standards — professional, social, sexual and educational standards. But where is our real worth? Is it not within us?

A Course In Miracles teaches we are all one — all equal in the love of God. It is necessary to push aside all the standards of the world and see ourselves as teachers of love with a clear message to bring to others. When we live in love we project a loving message, one we did not write. When we live in love it is God's message that others see in us.

Gerald Jampolsky wrote in *Teach Only Love:*

> Each of us to experience peace must recognize that we have a choice as to whether to view our identity as small and severely limited or as unlimited as love. . . . Love is the part of us that is real. It is the absence of fear and the recognition of complete union with all life. . . . Teach only love, for that is what you are.

Teaching To Learn

When I started writing I didn't concern myself with the progress of my writing; I simply turned it over to God, asking Him to put the right people in my path.

At first I wrote about teaching and education. I couldn't see the way I was headed. My addiction led me to study about addiction, and those studies led me to many articles and books that helped along the way. Through a series of coincidences — the right editor and the right publisher, just at the right moment — I have been guided in my endeavors.

There has always been a spiritual side to my message, so I often wonder about my adequacy in assuming the role of teacher in these issues. However, *A Course In Miracles* has taught me to regard myself as a teacher — without worrying about every word I speak. Now I realize that the words are written in my heart and it is my job to give them to those for whom they are intended — just as every person I meet is *my* teacher, with words for me.

One of the most profound messages I ever heard was in a half-way house for women who were homeless and in the early stages of recovery from alcoholism. I had just spoken, and in the discussion that followed a young woman who was just getting sober spoke up. "I ain't got nothin' but if I drink I ain't gonna be nothin'," she said. I never forgot the power of her words and the love of self that was projected from those words.

So it is that the power of God, of love itself, sustains us through times of fear if we choose to use that power. I can connect to that love and wisdom anytime or I can stay stuck in denial and self-pity. Letting go of the victim role is making a conscious decision to accept my true nature as a child of God. Does it take discipline? Yes! Does it take a new perspective? Yes! Does it take great courage? Yes! Does it take God's help? Yes!

Although it is the simplest and most natural concept — our return to our spiritual selves — it is not an easy journey. My human nature crowds in at times, telling me I can't possibly make it and I become terrified. My ego tells me I am alone. But somehow I connect to God again.

Think of what you could do with your life if you really believed that you are always safe in God's loving arms. If you believed that you were meant to be peaceful and living in a loving place all the time. That kind of living is from the power of God's love. All you have to do is reach within for that power and let it propel you to a better life.

Co-creating Love
Relationships

Co-creating in relationships means taking responsibility for our part in that joining. We become co-creators with the infinite spirit of a loving world, relating freely and truthfully. Truth brings trust, tolerance and forgiveness. That is living in love.

How many relationships are really spiritual? Really mature? Positive? Loving? It seems few intimate relationships are really loving; few families are really love-producing units. We all have special relationships that mean more to us than others. However, the way we behave within special relationships seems to indicate that many connections produce anything but love and spiritual growth. Perhaps we need to concentrate more on "co-creating love" by taking responsibility for our part in those relationships.

It is not surprising that so many relationships fail because a relationship is only as strong as its weakest partner. If both partners are not fully spiritual, the relationship is limited spiritually. Without this spiritual dimension, a relationship eventually falters.

At one time, I experienced a spiritual disquietude that just seemed to nag at me. For a time I filled that void with alcohol, then with people and, finally, with worldly possessions and recognition. Nothing worked until I turned my life and my will over to the care of God and began to make conscious contact with Him through prayer and meditation. This transformation left me more at peace inside. The nagging disquietude inside eased. No longer do I find I must have certain people, places and things in my life to be happy. Peace of mind and love were outside of me until I worked the 12 Steps and studied *A Course In Miracles*. Slowly I learned that love was inside and that "God is the love in which I live."

What is wrong with relationships today is what is wrong with our society in general. Most people have a tendency to reach outside of themselves to the material world to get the love and happiness that only the spiritual, immaterial world can give. Our thought system is ego-based rather than love-based.

In his book *Healing The Addictive Mind*, Lee Jampolsky states that all recovery from addiction is a process of "awakening to love." I believe it is learning to live in love, to co-create in relationships rather than being co-dependently driven by ego-centered thinking.

When we are ego-oriented, we think of ourselves as separate entities. We have to fight for every scrap of love we can get; we have to judge others so that we will seem better, more lovable; we worry about the past and present, and fear everyone and everything. However, when our thought system is love-based, everything changes. *A Course In Miracles* teaches us that we are all the same, whole and perfect children of God. We remain perfect even when our behavior is not. As the *Course* says, God could not create unequal beings. At our very spiritual core, we are all forgiven and equal in the love of God. For that reason, there is no need to judge others harshly but a need to accept them as they are. There is no reason to be afraid because we are always loved.

By changing the perspective of both partners in an intimate relationship, you change the relationship from co-dependency to co-creation. Co-dependency in a relationship indicates an ego-oriented thought system that produces dependent partners who absorb each other, stunt each other's spiritual growth and generate negative energy. Co-creation produces partners who are independent, existing in the same loving space and time, helping each other and others to grow spiritually and generating positive energy.

Before intimate partners can co-create love, they need to see their connection to love itself. Both partners must see themselves as children of God, as they really are, before they can move into co-creation.

So much of what we allow to happen to us is controlled by our view of what we are. If I am relating to you and you treat me with disrespect or discount me, I will allow that negative behavior to repeat itself only if I see myself as less than you. If I am complete in myself, unafraid of being alone, then I will not stay in a negative relationship just to be connected; or in the hope that things will get better; or with the belief that I will never find love again. If I am of God, or love itself, I know love is abundant and always available to me — alone or with you. Or with the very next person I meet. Love never ends — it is always available.

Undoing

Part of the process of building healthy relationships is an *undoing* — a complete change in perspective. First, I must see myself and others as God's holy children. Then I must live with that in mind.

When you meet anyone, remember, it is a holy encounter. As you see him, you will see yourself.

The second step in discovering love in relationships comes when we lose fear of others by seeing them as we see ourselves. As a result, we do not make their feelings, priorities, interests or decisions less than ours. We look inside the person rather than outside to see who they are. We respect their sadness or anger as their own and allow them to feel it. We respect their right to choose a different path or partner.

We are all children of light and it is our job to look for the light in each person we meet. This light is the energy of love. When we can't see the light in their behavior, we need to understand it is hidden under fear or anger. Perhaps their behavior is a cry for love.

Finally, if we are to relate in a loving way, we need to claim responsibility for our relationships. Not 50 percent as it has been suggested in popular self-help books, but 100 percent. Whenever there is total responsibility, there is health. I am the only one who can make me happy and I am responsible for what I choose in life — 100 percent responsible!

Special Relationships — Co-dependency

Before we look at the commitments needed to co-create love in relationships, let us review co-dependency and dispel the myths inherent in those relationships. Most co-dependents would say that their relationships are special and that they enter into the relationship 100 percent. In some ways, that is more than true and even seems to be the very problem. Co-dependents take 200 percent responsibility for their relationship. That is, they own their "stuff" and their partner's "stuff." That kind of obsessive control does not allow for freedom and flexibility.

Whenever I became obsessively concerned with another person, I allowed that person to become part of my identity. Therefore, it became necessary for me to be responsible for him as well as myself. What he did, or did not do, should not have affected me, but in fact it had a profound effect on me. He was me — we were one — in the most destructive, confining way possible. That is not love.

Co-dependency haunted and controlled me. I would reach out trying to control others so that I would not be controlled emotionally. We became enmeshed — the freedom ended, the flexibility was gone, the spiritual growth dwindled and I felt smothered and lost.

It doesn't matter if co-dependency occurs with an intimate partner, a child, a parent, a co-worker or a friend. It involves trying to own other people, trying to live their lives according to your plan and giving yourself up to your own obsession. The question is why? Why do I need someone else to make me whole?

Co-dependency is dangerous because it constricts spiritual growth and denies us the happiness of inner peace.

A Course In Miracles teaches me that the basic beliefs of co-dependency are false. They are my own misperceptions of the world in which we live, ego-based thoughts that lead to addictive thinking.

Ego-based beliefs tell me there is a scarcity of love so I'd better do everything I can to get love and to keep it. Co-dependence supports those beliefs. The root of the scarcity principle lies in the belief that we are spiritually empty. This empty place needs to be filled with love.

When I accept my role as a child of God, I see that I am of love itself and understand that place inside is already filled with God's love and grace. Existing through another person's love is no longer necessary. If I turn to God for help, I am given the miracle of light, the awareness to see what I am — a child of God, made in His image, made of love itself.

Co-dependent Misperceptions

The basic beliefs of co-dependence are wrong. They are misperceptions about our true nature, about the true nature of others, the world itself and the way we build relationships in it. Living in love is about changing these perceptions and changing the way we think.

Others may have their own spiritual journeys to complete, but for me the words of *A Course In Miracles* were the miracles of light, the points of awareness that brought me through this dark time. Since I believed I was alone in a terrifying world, I was frightened and controlled by co-dependency. Nothing seemed to help. Even though love was all around me, I believed that if one person did not love me, then I was unlovable. I lived in the past and projected into the future, made judgments about everyone around me and, out of fear, I tried to control the situation.

What I needed to do was identify the source of my fear, talk about my feelings, identify the negative self-talk within me and change it with new ideas, new words and a

whole new perspective. *A Course In Miracles* became a part
of my life at that time. The timing was most fortuitous.

Each day I read powerful meditations which slowly
changed my thought patterns. I attended a study of the
lessons and went to meetings where the *Course* was read
aloud and discussed.

When my co-dependent relationship ended, I was devastated. I continually examined the past to see where I
had gone wrong, and projected my fears into the future.
Then I read:

> *Everytime we become preoccupied with the future, we*
> *are creating an obstacle for love.*
> *Love lives in the present moment, absent of the past or*
> *the future.*

Because I kept returning to the past, it was very difficult to co-create love in a relationship in the present. I had
little chance to move out of that "stuck place" to a freer,
loving relationship.

So I judged myself negatively. I must be incapable of
love — it was all my fault. Back and forth I went in my
thoughts.

By choosing to experience conflict, I sabotaged every
relationship I entered. Love brings love. I was afraid of
love and I hadn't forgiven myself. First, I had to offer
forgiveness to myself, and then I could offer it to my
partner. That was the turning point which set me free to
love again. *A Course In Miracles* taught me:

> *When I have forgiven myself and remembered who I*
> *am, I will bless everyone and everything I see.*

Today I look to a partner who does not fill some empty
void inside of me, making me whole. Today I travel with
a partner whose light shines bright beside me. Together
we light the world.

Today I am thankful for any co-dependent relationships that I have endured because those people were my teachers. Learning from these relationships has brought me to real love and an understanding of how destructive this false kind of love can be. These special relationships were dangerous to my spiritual health. Guilt and fear dominated them; attack and defense became my only safety; mistakes called for judgment and punishment, not correction and learning; and the past and future robbed me of the present. I was afraid 100 percent of the time. I allowed my partner to determine my experience, my happiness and my self-worth. Since I thought I could control others, I lost sight of controlling my own thoughts, beliefs, feelings and behavior.

I was not happy in co-dependency because I chose not to be happy, because I acted defensively even though I yearned to be loving and loved. The only message I ever really wanted to say was, "Love me!" but I never did communicate that message. My partner, who was not spiritually mature enough to hear my underlying message, believed he was alone. He was afraid and dealt with the past and the future, and made judgments. His only message was "Love me!" but when I did not hear that message, he moved on to the next co-dependency.

Moving on to another partner never works until we change our perspective. That is not to say we can't correct a special co-dependent relationship. We can. If both partners get healthy and are willing to change their ego-based thinking, a holy relationship can develop. All things can be healed. However, it takes work and the grace of miracles. It means turning over the relationship to the Holy Spirit so that divine work can be done within that framework.

A Course In Miracles has taught me that all seemingly impossible things are in truth possible.

Conscious Commitments To
Co-Creating Love

Co-creating love in relationships involves some conscious commitments, ones that are usually difficult to undertake and difficult to maintain. These positive commitments are the polar opposites of the negative attitudes associated with co-dependency.

Openness

The first commitment to a healthy relationship is the commitment to openness. In *Conscious Loving*, Gay and Kathlyn Hendricks wrote:

> The only way to deepen and go forward in a close relationship is through becoming 'transparent.'

Becoming transparent comes from a conscious decision to reveal yourself to your partner.

If one partner is committed to revealing and the other committed to concealing, an imbalance occurs. To obtain perfect freedom and closeness, both people have to make a conscious decision to reveal themselves to the other. Partners might not be willing to commit to openness from fear of rejection, need to control or the need to deceive. If both people are serious and capable of contributing to a healthy relationship, they must be willing to be open — transparent.

A commitment to openness can come only when we know and love ourselves. In an open relationship, it is okay to be as we really are because fear is not shutting us down. Our partners encourage us by being as they are. We will never be known and loved if we don't dare to open ourselves to others. Once there is nothing to hide, we can be free to live in love.

Honesty

The second commitment to a healthy relationship is honesty. Openness and honesty are not necessarily the same. Being willing to open myself up to another human being has to do with the sharing of "self," while being honest has to do with keeping agreements and being responsible for my own actions.

Keeping agreements, large and small, is very important in any relationship because it nourishes the trust between partners. Without trust, the relationship falters and sometimes fails. Agreements can be broken unintentionally — like being late for an appointment, always late for dinner or not calling when you say you will. These are little agreements but they send a powerful message to our partner. Either I am honest or I'm not. There is no in between. When I say I will do something, be someplace or make a call, I must make every effort to carry it through. Otherwise my partner has a right to question my honesty. Other more serious pledges of fidelity and loyalty can be questioned when smaller agreements are broken consistently.

When I break an agreement, I need to tell the truth and make amends promptly. If I find this difficult to do, I may be hiding anger towards my partner or the relationship itself. This anger will have to be dealt with in time. Keep your promises and you will be trusted. Tell the truth at all times, even when it is not convenient or is embarrassing, and you will be believed.

Honesty hinges on keeping agreements and owning your own actions. Being responsible for my actions, completely responsible, helps to co-create a loving relationship. It helps me create my own world, build my own reality. I need to understand that I am totally responsible for my actions because I choose what I do and what I don't do. I choose to be happy and accept the vagaries of life or I choose to be a victim and to blame others.

I have stressed the sickness of choosing to relate co-dependently. Looking back at the sickness of those harmful relationships is part of recovery. Those relationships brought me to health. But first I had to get honest and admit my part in that dysfunction.

A healthy relationship is possible only when both partners are capable of owning their "own stuff" and not projecting blame on others. When "your stuff" harms others, you need to acknowledge it, make amends and change it.

In *Conscious Loving*, Gay and Kathlyn Hendricks tell us:

> Co-dependence ends the moment you interrupt an argument and say, "I'm willing to own how I have created this situation in my life." Co-commitment begins the moment the other person says, "I'm also willing to find out how I have created it." Co-dependence is two people fighting over who is responsible. Co-commitment is two people agreeing that each is 100 percent responsible.

The world we experience is the effect of our own thoughts. Relationships go bad when we expect our partners to perceive and react as we do. Then our ego-based thinking tells us we are separate and we may give up on the whole idea of love. In reality, we are all one in love itself, in God.

Communication

Communication is the third commitment for all healthy relationships. There are many ways to say "I love you," whether we specifically state our feelings or imply it in our actions. So much of what we think and feel is transmitted to others by our body language, our smile and our general attitude. Wishing to communicate in a loving way is half the process, but loving communication can't be faked or forced. The first person I have to love is me and when I do, I will be able to project that love outside of myself to my partner.

Being present in the moment helps me to communicate love in relationships. When I see things through the eyes of the past or project into the future, I lose the moment.

We can't hear each other when we let the past or future interfere.

Communication takes sensitivity. It isn't all talking; it is also listening and learning. If you know your partner well, you can communicate more fully.

Knowing how and when to touch in a loving way, in a sexual way, in a way of simple support is a learned act. Partners need to be willing to express their wants and needs and to share their feelings, not withhold affection or loving thoughts and actions from their partner. Continual positive communication is essential to any relationship.

To be able to communicate to others, I first need to understand what I need, want and feel. Once again, self-knowledge and self-love come into play. It takes time to be able to recognize what I feel. For example, am I depressed because I'm angry about something that has happened in the relationship? Am I angry at someone else because I'm really angry at myself? Do I need to express that anger? How? When? Where? Am I reacting to old traumas or is there really something wrong in the relationship today?

Seeking out the source of our feelings takes a willingness to be real. Finding the proper way to express feelings in an appropriate way, time and place takes determination and skill in interpersonal relating. Therapists and others in 12-Step programs can help us improve communication skills if we feel inadequate in that area. However, the most important thing is a willingness to admit to the problem and to learn how to correct it, a determination to continue to communicate when things seem futile and the intuition to know when it is no longer necessary to communicate. There are times when partners need to work through their own feelings.

Involvement

The fourth commitment in a co-creative relationship is involvement. You can't create unless you relate. Love al-

ways implies action and energy. It may be that your loved
one is not near you but you can transmit powerful messages of love by thinking of them. Love implies connection.

Any interpersonal relationship requires investment. It
means time, energy, money and concentration. Without
effort, a relationship will die. Selfish people have a hard
time investing in an ongoing relationship. Living in love
makes demands on us, but we always get back what we
give in love.

Over the last four years, my immediate family has had
the gift of unity and love. With me, with my children and
with the father of these children there has been a magnif-
icent co-creation of relationship — a functioning family.
When members needed special help, everyone rallied to
their side. There has been little conflict and a wonderful
energy that flows within the family. Our original family
group was torn apart by alcoholism, but with all members
in recovery there is a spiritual growth that is easy for
others to see, and for us, as members, to feel. We know
we have something very special because we are told that
we do, and we can feel it.

When my children's father was told that he had a limited
time to live, we became stronger as a group. Even though
we were no longer legally married, we remained father
and mother with our family reunited and functioning in
love and compassion. Holidays, weddings, births, college
acceptances — all were shared with joy. Others looked on
in amazement. Living in love gets the attention of others.

Two months ago my children lost their father and our
family lost an important member. In the months before he
died, there was honesty and sharing, and in the moment
of death we were able to be present in strength, peace and
love. There is no greater gift we could have given to each
other and to him. But the wonderful part is that we all
knew what a special family we had become.

We continue to share honestly and openly. All of my children spoke at the funeral service with great respect for their father. It was clear that where one member of our group moved, the others followed. It was clear that forgiveness and love had melded our family into a very powerful force. One of my greatest gifts from God has been this functioning family, this communication within the family — father, mother, child, child, child. Now with one member physically gone, we still function with his presence remembered. So adept at relating together, we have grown capable of being there for each other, of doing for each other and of recognizing the loss in the family. Love never ends. It continues to heal and soothe, even after the spirit has left the body. A loving family remains a loving family even when they lose a loved one.

Productivity

The fifth commitment partners need to make is the commitment to develop their God-given gifts to their fullest. When one partner is unproductive or unmotivated, he or she will draw on the resources of others. Inequality will destroy the balance of a relationship and eventually kill it.

Addiction in a relationship creates havoc. When there is addiction present, it's like having a thief in the house. There is no winning with this intruder because it generates fear, destroys love and keeps both partners from developing their God-given potentials. Therefore, the relationship never develops fully.

Even in a relationship without serious hindrances such as addiction, it is difficult to stay focused enough to grow spiritually. You might ask how one can communicate, make an investment and be involved in the relationship and still have time to develop one's gifts? It demands a delicate balance. Nevertheless, if I work 100 percent to be close in a relationship, and 100 percent to develop my gifts, I will find the time and energy for both commitments.

With understanding comes empowerment of each other. It means supporting partners in being their best, and in finding and using their God-given talents. It means meeting partners on a spiritual level. Relationships don't just provide us with compassion, attention, sex, material goods and support; they also empower us spiritually, enabling us to give love to others and to be happy within ourselves.

Joy

The sixth commitment in co-creating love is to be happy. "God's will for me is joy." It is my responsibility to accept that joy into my relationship, into my life. The world will always be full of inconsistencies, tragedies and dilemmas, but my task is to be happy. It is a clear choice we all make — to be victims or to prevail. My happiness depends on whether I accept what life brings or stay stuck in resentment and self-pity. Accepting uncertainties within a relationship is my responsibility. Even in the worst situation, there is something to be grateful for. Having a positive outlook, having fun, doing the things that nourish me — these are my responsibilities. If I choose to be unhappy, I will be. No one can make me happy or unhappy. That's up to me.

Health

Finally, the co-creation of love involves a commitment to our own physical and spiritual health. We need to eat right, take care of our bodies, exercise and be all that we can be physically. In addition, we need to take care of our spirits with loving attention to ourselves as God's children. I have spoken of the importance of the spiritual side of life which I believe is attained by accepting that we are God's children, living a life that matches that role, recognizing the essence of love in others, forgiving ourselves and others, finding the power of love within ourselves and using that power to enter relationships in a new, loving way.

Caring for ourselves physically and spiritually is a most precious and serious commitment because when we are physically and spiritually fit, we are better equipped to do the work of relating. Under these circumstances, we can find the needed confidence to move within the relationship. We can adjust to changes necessary for growth. We can always look within to find the power to live in love.

Co-creating love is a mystery, a miracle of two physical beings joining spiritually. It takes great deliberation, yet it takes none. It is a question that was answered before it was asked. It is hope, courage, silence, faith and commitment. It is everything there is to know and yet it is already known.

Holy Relationships

Co-creating love is not confined to the standard types of societal relationships. *A Course In Miracles* speaks of the difference between "special relationships," which are limited and co-dependent, and "holy relationships," which are not restricted.

A Course In Miracles explains that a "special" or "unholy" relationship is based on differences because each partner thinks the other has what he or she does not. They come together to take from each other.

A "holy" relationship starts from a different place. As each partner has searched within, they have found they are not lacking. They both accept their spirituality; they are children of God. This acceptance of the whole self helps one to join with another who is a whole, perfect spiritual being. That joining is a holy relationship.

It took me a couple of years to entertain the possibility of merit in this kind of thinking. In a co-dependent relationship that appears to be "very special," I might favor one person to the exclusion of all others. But how do we know who God is using to teach us love if we are not open to all people at all times? It could be one chance meeting, one flashing "holy instant" that teaches us of love.

I remember a day early in my recovery when I was feeling depressed and ungrateful. Thank God days like those are rare now. However, on that day God put in my path a young girl whose image I shall never forget. Her face was so disfigured that it would be difficult to describe it. I still remember the purple color and rough skin. As I was going into church, I saw her standing by the door. It was a momentary meeting but a shock went through me like lightning. I was stunned. I cried as I knelt and thanked God for His blessings. How could I allow myself to disfigure myself inside with ingratitude and unhappiness when I was normal outside. How much harder it was for this girl to greet the world each day. God teaches me through other people, and sometimes it is the handicapped who have become my dearest teachers.

We learn from all relationships and find moments of wonder and glory in unusual places. Just when we look the other way for a minute, someone very special will show up and teach us what we need to learn. Trying to seek special relationships and special moments comes from ego-based thinking.

A Course In Miracles teaches us that every encounter we enter is a holy encounter. It can be one either of fear or love. It is up to us. If we are negative, unforgiving and judgmental, then the basis is fear. If we are positive, forgiving and nonjudgmental, or at-one with others, we are living in love. Therefore, we teach either love or fear.

When we come from love, we will be at peace, which is our ultimate goal. Or when the ego dominates, we will be in conflict, which, at best, distracts us from life and love. Each one of us has the opportunity to surrender each holy encounter of each day to the Holy Spirit. Turn it all over to God. Don't even try to manage it yourself.

People who make us angry or upset for any reason are our most important teachers. They mirror what is in us. If I see anger, then I am angry. If I cannot forgive, it is because I have not forgiven myself. Some people say they need to correct people and define their boundaries. That is true to a certain degree because if we are God's children, we don't deserve abuse and don't have to accept it. Nevertheless, we don't need to assign guilt — and thus reinforce our own guilt.

Forgiveness is letting go and seeing anew. It is finding the commonality in all of us. Only love is real and only loving encounters matter.

I am reminded of this each year as I start my school year. Inevitably, there will be boys and girls so starved for love that they become discipline problems to get attention, using abusive language, being loud and unruly.

I remember Billy, a tall, good-looking senior who appeared to be tough and mean. Billy had disruption down to a science. He would interrupt people, burp, make uncalled-for comments and make faces in class. I complied with his desire for attention and sent him to the principal's office.

On his third trip to the office, as he left the room, he said, "I was just trying to break my record. Last year's English teacher threw me out 33 times." I thought about that and decided to stop throwing him out. I began "to teach only love." When he was abusive, I went up to him and in a loving voice corrected him. He didn't know what to do with the love. This might have been the first time anyone treated him that way.

As the year progressed, Billy was allowed to read Stephen King in an independent reading program. He devoured the books and remained quiet in class. When I went to The American Booksellers Association Convention that year, I told Stephen King's publisher about Billy and he sent copies of his latest books. Billy was impressed.

The turning point came when I did a positive affirmations exercise with the class. Each student was supposed to list ten positive things about another student. No one picked Billy, so I made up his list. He watched me write: 1. tall, 2. good-looking, 3. nice smile, 4. dark hair, 5. loyal, 6. persistent, 7. loves to read, 8. beautiful face, 9. dark eyes, 10. never forgets. When I was done, he smiled and said, "How did you know that stuff." I said, "I just know, Billy." Teaching is not all English — it is love.

It was true Billy was a terrible student — undisciplined, rude and disrespectful. But I asked God to let me see him differently through the eyes of love rather than fear. By changing my perception of him, I changed his of himself. It is like that — love generates love. We give love to others so that we can remain at peace within. I didn't let Billy run rampant over the class as he tested my authority in the early days of the class. When it was appropriate, I switched and let love in — not out of weakness but out of strength. There is the difference. Many people think it is weak to act defenseless but, at appropriate times, defenselessness shows great power. Living in love looks passive sometimes but it generates a lasting energy.

A year ago when I was visiting my son in Malibu, California, I had a "holy instant." It involved Chester, a homeless man who lives on the beach amidst multimillion dollar homes. My son pointed him out to me as he was making his morning run on the beach. Chester was tanned, fit and looked to be in his early thirties. There was something very different about him — he exuded an almost pristine naturalness. I wondered if I would see him again.

I did. It was a chance meeting in the Malibu public library. Every day Chester sits in the same seat in the reading room of the library. He reads about metaphysics. He believes that children lose their self-esteem at the hands of unattentive, neglectful parents. Chester doesn't believe in unconditional love; he thinks humans are often evil.

With his jacket hung over the library chair, to hide his water bottle and bagel with cream cheese, he sits with his homemade radio transmitter reading about the mysteries of the world.

He greeted me politely and spoke of the writer John Wise. "Perhaps you remember his name. Dolphins? He wrote about dolphins?" he asked.

I nodded and said, "Yes, they talk to each other."

"I'd like to listen to some of those tapes that have sub-liminal messages like, *How To Have Confidence* or *Self-Esteem*. That is my next step," he said enthusiastically, gesturing toward a book on the library table that he needed to finish. I assumed he would learn more from tapes when he was done with metaphysics.

We talked about how people seem not to see the home-less. He shut his eyes when he said, "They do not see me because they are blind." He held his head up high, keeping his eyes shut.

"Blind," he said. "They are all blind! If they see us, they will have to admit this is happening." When he opened his eyes, I realized that they were beautiful.

I asked him if he ever wrote down his ideas in a journal and he said he had "no place to keep it." He seemed baffled by my question. When I offered him money, he was of-fended and refused saying, "I don't take charity." Once again, I noticed his eyes. He wouldn't be compromised or bought, and he didn't believe in illusions.

Chester had what I imagine to be the vision of Christ in his eyes — all that is innocent, all that is painful. A burning light.

I said, "You have beautiful eyes."

He said very simply, "No one ever said that before." I was glad to have been able to.

At the Los Angeles airport, I waited to board my plane to Connecticut. So powerful was my impression of Chester that I needed to record the incident, so I wrote as I waited. Some travelers from France were excitedly speaking in broken English to anyone who would listen. Chester said that he never speaks to anyone. An officious, offensive businessman with an impeccably tailored suit was speaking loudly to another man, also impeccably dressed in a tailored suit, about profit, loss and 10 percent dividends. Chester has no money nor will he accept any. Chester has no place to keep what he records so he keeps it all within himself.

I thought of him as he was about to leave the library, to go home to his place beside a fence. He will set up his towels to make a tent and be glad they are dry. Perhaps he will remember me and think of some of the things we said. Then he will run the length of the beach and people from the decks of their multimillion dollar homes will yell, "Hi, Chester!" And tonight he will sleep with the sound of the ocean pounding on the shore — and his spirit will be free. Perhaps more than yours or mine.

The holy moments we encounter in our everyday life provide a spiritual connection with others. They start with the recognition that each moment of each day is precious and each person we meet unique. When we are living in love, we understand love is everywhere. It is an inexhaustible commodity. All we need to do is tap into it.

Co-creating relationships challenges us to commit to love in every aspect of our living. It brings us back to the God in us and in all others. It asks us to live by our true spiritual nature, by love itself.

The Power Of Words

7

There is a power in the written and spoken word — great power. Start to listen to what you say to others. Then listen to your inner voice. What do you hear? Is it love, resentment, anger, forgiveness or hatred? What is your message?

A Course In Miracles has taken its place among the world's great expressions of spiritual truth, such as the *Bible,* the *Koran,* the *Talmud* and the *I Ching.* The words of the *Course* open the heart to healing and hope, to enlightenment and to love. When reading the words of the *Course,* a great spiritual power seems to embrace us and bring us home.

Marianne Williamson wrote this in the foreword of *Accept This Gift* by Frances Vaughan and Roger Walsh:

> For me, and for thousands, perhaps millions of other people, *A Course In Miracles* is a miracle in itself — paragraph after paragraph of words that change our minds. Where we viewed the world through the eyes of fear, suddenly we see new hope revealed. Reading we are startled by its simplicity and awed by the scope of its promise . . . we are in the process, through exposure to these ideas on whatever level, of tranforming our lives from fear to love.

A Course In Miracles is a cultural and publishing phenomenon. Since its publication in 1976, nearly 1,000,000 copies have been sold. Not through the promotion of a major publisher but through word of mouth. Dr. Helen Schucman, an educator at a prestigious New York university, is said to have been the scribe for this channeled work, which is comprised of a text, a workbook for students and a manual for teachers. The workbook includes 365 lessons — one for each day of the year.

Tara Singh whose work, *A Course In Miracles: A Gift For All Mankind* says:

> *A Course In Miracles* is the first scripture to offer a step-by-step curriculum for undoing the patterns of thought which keep us separated from God, ourselves and each other.

A Course In Miracles challenges us to tranform the way we perceive everything and everyone — including ourselves. It helps us undo everything that blinds us to our own perfection. Its words bring us love. Love is a state unaffected by words but words can direct us to it. There is great power in words.

Much of my experience with the *Course* has been an assimilation of words in stillness and peace, with no expectation of learning. It is therefore difficult to write about. Spiritual words defy analysis because they stand on their own. They heal and free us by igniting our spirits to awareness — staying within us, breathing for us, touching others with their peace and gentleness and allowing us to internalize our true identities as children of God.

Wherever I read in the *Course*, I am moved to the spiritual place I need to be. If you have experienced that in reading quotations from the *Course* in this book, you can appreciate the power of the entire work. The *Course's* three volumes provide a lifetime of assimilation, of consumption, of translation into our everyday lives.

A Course In Miracles relates to us directly, addressing the yearning in each of us to know God, to know truth and to know peace and love. It challenges us to undo the past, to release its hold on us.

The words of *A Course In Miracles* help to liberate us from a materialistic, ego-centered thought system and bring us a new consciousness. This consciousness tells me I do not have to depend on others, that my awakening begins within. I am sustained by the love of God. I learn to say: "God is the mind in which I think. God is the love with which I live."

Through *A Course In Miracles*, I have come to know perfection — my own divine perfection as a child of God. I find freedom in that realization — a freedom that brings the stillness of a mind at peace.

Teach Only Love

The Introduction to *A Course In Miracles* states:

> This Course does not aim at teaching the meaning of love, for that is beyond what can be taught. It does aim, however, at removing the blocks to the awareness of love's presence, which is your natural inheritance.

As the words of *A Course In Miracles* have reached me, I have reached out to share with you what I have experienced through the *Course*. It is an ongoing cycle because love never ends.

Words are the spiritual tools for all teachers. We are told in the words of the *Course* that we are messengers teaching either love or fear. We will extend to others what we perceive within:

> *Everyone teaches and teaches all the time. This is the responsibility you inevitably assume the moment you accept any premise at all, and no one can organize his life without some thought system. Once you have developed a thought system of any kind, you live by it, and you teach it.*

I believe we teach with our words as well as with our actions. Much of the psychic pain I experience comes when my words and actions are not congruent. It is impossible to see myself as a child of God when I persist in harming myself and others. Our words and our actions need to be in sync for us to get a clear view of our real spiritual selves. Words and actions are the vehicles of our message to those around us — a message of love or fear.

Learning and teaching are one. I could not write this book had I not first experienced the words of *A Course In Miracles*. The love of those words transformed my thinking so that, in the words of Step 2, I "came to believe." The *Course* says to "remember always what you believe you will teach." Then, as we teach, we strengthen our

beliefs in the sharing of them. The *Course* says: "Everything you teach you are learning. Teach only love, and
learn that love is yours and you are love." I try to teach
only love because I believe that I am God's child, that I
come from love itself!

Is it possible to "teach only love"? Yes. When we are
wronged, misled or unjustly treated, it is difficult to be
loving. However, love does not have to be spoken quietly.
Sometimes it can come in the form of strong words spoken with firmness. It can be loving to tell someone to
leave you or that you must leave them. It can be loving to
say, "I cannot support you in this behavior any longer." It
can be loving to say, "This is not a holy, loving relationship
but a sick, dependent one." It can be loving to stop "people-
pleasing," to stop "enabling" others, to stop giving approval
to unacceptable behavior. Teaching love does not imply
weakness, but strength.

A Course In Miracles made me realize the power of words,
not only in the spiritual sense but in every other sense.
Realizing how I have changed as a result of the message of
A Course In Miracles, I came to understand the power of
words in my everyday encounters with others. Since we
can't always see the physical damage done by words, we
sometimes forget their force, either positive or negative.

How often do we remember an expression of love that
we have heard? How often do we hear from others that
they appreciated our words of encouragement or praise?
Words are powerful because they can bring love. Just as
the *Course* brings me words of love that I can internalize,
so too can I bring words of love to others. It can be a
simple expression of patient understanding to a hurried
clerk in a store, or the words "I love you" spoken to a
loved one. Words are conveyors of love or fear.

So we need to look at what we say. We need to respect
our verbal power and use it carefully. Ridicule, derision
and sarcasm are words of the ego. They say, "I am right

and you are wrong." "I am more, you are less." "I am afraid of you, so I will make you less than me." Words hurt! Negative words can separate and destroy the loving spirits of others.

In co-creating love within personal relationships, it is wise to look at what you say. How do you sound? Loving? Fearful? Righteous? What is your agenda? What do your words really mean? Listen to what you say and you will establish where you are spiritually.

Ego-Based Thinking

When we use words to teach fear, we are operating from ego-based thinking. Our ego tells us we are alone in a frightening world and we need to do everything possible to protect ourselves from harm. When someone attacks us, we retaliate with words; we strike back at the mind of the attacker with hateful, angry words. In those instances, we are teaching fear, isolation and hatred. Attacking anyone at any time with words is an ego-based position of defense which says, "You are not stronger than I am." "You can not harm me!" Defensive words may seem appropriate and necessary at times but, in truth, they serve no useful purpose.

Our illusion is that we are weak and defenseless but in reality we are strong. We are God's children.

Without illusions there could be no fear, no doubt and no attack.

There is great power in defenselessness. The *Course* repeats this message many times: "In my defenselessness my safety lies." Because we are spiritual beings, made by God to teach only love, we have no need of verbal attack or attacking thoughts.

When we use words to harm, we show that we do not believe we are all equal in God's love. There is no need for words of ridicule, sarcasm or derision. These words will not change the spiritual value of anyone. The ego evaluates and tries to make less or more, but love makes one.

Listen to the words you speak. Do you attack? Do you brag? Do you put others down? Do you criticize?

Words that sound loving are not always based in love. Since words are powerful, people can use them to project love when they are really trying to control or deceive. Flattery that is misused and kind words not meant in kindness are lies with a loving aura. These words come from the dark place of fear. It is an empty soul that pretends to love in order to be loved. How desperately unworthy and alone we must feel when we think we have to bargain for or buy love with our words, with our behavior. We all deserve love without any conditions, without any reservations.

Love Words

There is great power and great danger in words. Listen carefully — they are not always what they seem to be. Our words can be cloaked in false pride, manipulation, righteousness and hidden anger. We can attempt to kill the loving spirit of another if we do not recognize our own loving spirit.

There are six attributes that come forth when we teach only love.

Patience

The first attribute is *patience*. Being patient in your words is an act of love. Listening to the message of others and taking time to hear each word is the patience of love. Answering carefully and with deliberation is love. So many words are misunderstood because they are abruptly spoken. Being considerate of the feelings of others by being patient is an act of love.

Kindness

Using words that we would like to hear shows *kindness* — the second attribute. We need to think of how our words are received. Are we gentle? Are we using endearments? Are we using words of love as we speak? Or are we bullying, berating and badgering people with words? Words can be kind and gentle, or harsh and cruel. We are the messengers. We need to keep asking ourselves, "What am I teaching?"

Respect

A third attribute of loving expression is *respect*. What is the tone of your voice? Are your words respectful of other people? Do we really respect their spirituality? Or do we discount them? Respect means equality — even if they are different, poor, handicapped or even if they attack you with harsh resentful words. The respect we hold for others shows in the way we speak to them.

Sincerity

A fourth attribute of loving expression is *sincerity*. Without sincerity, words become lies. There is no way that a person can judge whether your words are coming from love or fear. You are the source of those words — you are the only one who can know what is inside you. When you operate out of fear, you will lie; but when you are of love itself, a child of God, your fear will be gone and you will be able to love unconditionally. To teach only love is to respect the Godliness of the person to whom you communicate.

Recently at a 12-Step meeting, I sat next to a man who moved me to compassion. He was so thin and gaunt, it seemed as if his very bones would break out of his skin. His eyes were protuding from their sockets, his face grey and drawn. It was obvious that he was struggling, very near death after a long bout of disease, and that he did not have many days left. I felt the need to reach out and touch him. When the meeting was over, I stood up and hesitated, but I knew I had to speak to him. I turned to him and said,

"God be with you," and asked if I could hug him. He stood up and we hugged. His frail body seemed all bones. Then he thanked me for touching him. I understood. Once again, I said, "God be with you. God be with you." I know he knew I understood his fear and his isolation, and I knew he felt the sincerity of my words.

Humility

The fifth attribute of loving words is *humility*. I might have avoided this man out of a sense of false pride. Would he think me foolish? Would he think I pitied him? Was I trying to be a "do-gooder"? There is humility in the expression of loving words because sometimes we have to remove ourselves, our egos, from the situation and get completely outside ourselves. Sometimes we have to be humble enough to do something uncommon or risk rejection. When we humble ourselves by risking, we love. When we speak directly from the heart, from the soul, it might seem out of place, but it will be of love itself.

Generosity

The sixth attribute in loving expression is *generosity*. It takes selflessness to listen to the words of others and it takes time to respond. It takes a generous spirit to find the energy to communicate fairly and lovingly. How much easier it is to say, "You make me angry." How simple it is to blame someone else. How much more loving it is to claim the anger as yours and not accredit it to someone else. Loving words require a generosity, an owning up to the responsibility of our feelings and a generous release of all around us from that responsibility.

Generosity in loving words takes energy, concentration and time. Rather than reacting immediately to some affront, we need to think the situation through and stay with our own feelings. It takes time and energy to practice this type of response. Whenever you feel a surge of anger, let it be a warning bell. Concentrate. Why are you feeling this way? What has happened in the relationship that produced that anger? Own it! Speak about it or it will fester. Before we can deal with any emotion, we need to understand it. The last thing we need to do is transfer it to the closest person by saying, "You make me angry!"

Generous loving expression is not veiled in some hidden agenda. It is straightforward. It says, "I feel lonely today and I need you to stay with me for a few hours." It does not say, "What are you planning to do today? Where are you going now? Where will you be this afternoon?" Generous loving expression does not set traps so that our partners fall into saying the wrong thing. Generous loving expression tells the truth; it does not look for answers and it does not omit important information.

Words are instruments of spiritual destruction or spiritual growth. They can bring forth love or they can project fear. Some people think power is in fists, in bullets or in bombs. I believe it is in words. Not only can words shame a soul, pierce a mind or uplift the heart in a few seconds, but they can stay with you for a lifetime. We remember what others say to us. We remember.

Think back to the most important words you have heard. You know them. They are engraved on your heart and you can replay them at will. When you were seven years old and your cousin yelled at you for burning the pillowcase with the iron, you cringed in shame, never forgetting the feeling of failure. Ironing was her thing, she knew how to do it, you didn't and you made a terrible mistake. Later that day you ran away to a secret place and cried, wishing you could die because you were so ashamed. It was such a simple thing but her words never left your mind.

Remember the words of your mother when she said, "The doctor said it's malignant"? Yes, you remember the words, just as you remember the green corridors, the white-tiled floors, the doors that swung open and the sign, Maine General Hospital. Somehow, even at age 12, words like "malignant" never leave your mind.

You picked up the telephone and it was your mother's voice again. She said, "I have bad news. Michael is dead."

Then there was your husband, sitting by your bed with his hands holding his head waiting for you to wake up so he could say, "The baby is dead."

No one could have said words of more power. Such words get branded into our minds forever.

Do you remember the first time a boyfriend or girl-friend said, "I love you"? Do you remember your response? Do you remember a favorite fourth grade teacher who told you that you could write well or that you were creative? Not only are words the creators of love and confidence, they are the energy that allow us to continue to love, to work and to create. *We remember words.*

It is said that God works through others. Not only does God use our actions, but He uses our words. We can be teachers and lovers, or we can destroy with an attack and hatred. Sometimes words are so subtly spoken that they don't seem dangerous, but in time they erode confidence and spirit.

Unsolicited criticism is an attack because it is not specif-ically called for by the other person. There is no need to chance the damage of someone's spirit with well-meaning criticism.

Parents are the guardians of their child's delicate spirit. Parents need to look carefully at the words they speak in frustration and anger. Words can destory vulnerable little children. I cringe when I hear a mother say, "You are a bad boy. You never do anything right." I die inside when I hear an older sister telling a younger child, "You can't do that." Negative words cling like parasites and eventually corrupt the perception and performance of adults. You might think we would outgrow these words, but in our subcon-scious minds they lurk waiting to rise up and haunt us. If we could dismiss damaging words, wash them away like dirt, we would never have to face them, but we can't. Words are so powerful because they become imbedded in our minds, becoming part of our inner voice.

My father, an uneducated immigrant from Ireland, was a proud, hard-working man who loved children. The words of praise he used were coveted by all eight of us. We prized beyond measure the "darlins" and "dearies" that rolled off his Gaelic tongue. Like many of the Irish, he was a man of power when it came to words. My father loved to storytell, and his tales were rich with colorful details. It was a treat to be the subject of his story. However, if he was not proud of you or if he could not bring himself to praise, the silence was deadly. He never knew that his omission of words of acceptance and love with some of his children had harmed them for life. Nor could he anticipate that my life would be touched by men who were exactly like my father — men who were capable of endearments, men who charmed me with their words or devastated me with their silence.

The spoken word is a powerful instrument of love or fear. How we use words is up to us. Sometimes we are stripped of everything until there is nothing but the spoken word. I remember such a time.

Route 2 arched toward Concord, Massaschussets. She remembered the rotary and the ominous prison buildings on the right.

"My God," she said. "I remember the times we drove together by this place, over this road."

Remembering their college days, the football games at Boston College, the visits to his parents' home, Jenny forgot for a moment the reason for her trip today. Her thoughts went back instead to an arrogant mother-in-law who had never accepted Jenny, a father-in-law who had a loving heart, 17 years of marriage, three children and a bitter divorce due to the damage wrought by alcoholism.

Jenny sighed as she checked the road signs. Concord never changes, she thought, seeing the old colonial houses, painted white with black shutters, stately, hard to heat, with their widow's walks on the roofs. But this day was not for sightseeing.

"Someplace it should say Cameron Hospital," she said aloud.

Then she saw the sign with a big H on it and turned right. Another right and into the parking garage. She took a ticket and circled several times before finding an empty space. Anxious and frustrated, she walked briskly toward the gatekeeper.

Agitated, she muttered, "I can't imagine having to pay to go see someone in the hospital — maybe even die." The young attendant just shrugged her shoulders.

Once inside, Jenny waited impatiently as the elevator descended. She tried to put the years together. Their marriage ended fifteen years ago. There had been nine more years of alcoholism, sobriety and recovery and then four years of diabetes and cancer. And now, his imminent death.

They said the cancer was in his brain. How long can it be if that is true? She wondered, thinking that no one ever knows. She felt gratitude for the last four years of wonderful moments, for reconciliation, for the peace they had come to as a couple, as a family.

When Jenny walked into the room, she felt that something was terribly wrong. She knew immediately that he was dying. Her first thought was the children. Then she moved closer to the man who had given her those children, who had been her husband, and she held his hand as his whole body shook in the throes of death. It was as if his spirit was fighting to be released from his body — every spasmodic movement of his deteriorated body brought death one second closer. There was no time!

"Someone call the children — tell them there is no time — quickly!" she whispered so that he would not hear. Jenny remembered that her daughter had promised her father she would be with him at the end and knew she was driving there at this moment. She remembered the concern in her oldest son's voice when he said he would take the next flight. There was no time. She remembered the preoccupation of her youngest son just hours before as he hesitantly went to work. Above all, she knew that this dying man loved his children more than anything in the world and that they loved him. Then again, to the people in the room, "Hurry! Try to contact the children."

Back at his bedside, she held his hand and comforted him with her words.

"It is all right." she said. "You are all right." More moments of wracking pain. "The children are coming. They love you." He tried to speak but could not form the words with his parched mouth.

"I understand," she whispered. "I love you." She had not said that to him since the days of their marriage. He tried to respond but could not.

"I know," she said. "I understand." In a few moments his youngest son arrived, brought to his bedside simply by "sensing something was wrong and rushing over to the hospital." It was minutes before his death. In the end, the wracking movements of pain stopped as his skin turned yellow and blood trickled from his mouth. The usefulness of his body was over as his spirit departed. At that moment, his son touched his father's head and said, "Peace, Dad, peace." Jenny leaned in closer and whispered, "You can go now. It is okay. I will take care of the children. God will take you home. We will follow you!"

It was over. He was gone. In that instant, words were the last gift to be given to a loved one. They were the only gift that could be given.

Every day we have an opportunity to touch others with our words of love or to harm with words that produce fear and hatred. That is the challenge of living in love. To take the love from inside and give it to others. We may give material gifts to those we love but they will deteriorate with time, losing their value. Our words last forever.

The
Inner Voice

We have an inner voice that leads us to truth and love. All we have to do is find that voice within and, once fear and hatred are dispelled, we will be free to love. Positive affirmations remind us of who we are and help us to project positive messages to others. Changing our thinking changes our lives. Let your gentle, loving inner voice change you from the inside out.

Spoken words are important. What others say to us can affect us today and for years. Words can destroy or heal. We are subject to the power of words every day. Our spouse, our boss, our friends use this power on us. Mentally we take in those words and are hurt or healed by them. We have to respect the power of words and be prepared to deal with their effect on us.

Just as we can heal with our words, we can be healed by the words of others. Just as we can destroy with words, we can allow ourselves to be destroyed. Negative messages have a way of staying with us as they arise from the subconscious and plague us when we least expect it. Negative messages like these can become a part of our inner voice: "How could you do that? You're so stupid. Who do you think you are? You'll never succeed. You never get along with anyone. No one could ever love you. You're too fat. You're no good."

So what can we do about these negative messages? We have a choice. We can listen to the old outdated messages or we can reshape new positive ones. It takes reprogramming. Because our minds are like computers, they take in everything — the good and the bad. Messages are filed away to be brought up at will. All of what we have heard in the past is saved in our minds. However, we have the power to sort and delete messages; we have the power to control our minds. There is not much we can control in the world around us, but we can learn to be responsible for our inner talk.

Besides sorting and deleting, we have the power to create new files, ones that can be retrieved when we need to affirm our goodness, our love of self, our position as a child of God. We do not have to listen to a negative inner voice. In fact, it is our responsibility to switch files whenever we hear negative messages.

111

How do we do that? By making a conscious effort on a
daily basis to govern our inner voice. A two-step process
is involved here. First comes the positive inner affirmation; a positive attitude with positive actions will follow.
Whatever our inner voice tells us will be translated into
action. Negative talk equals negative action. Positive talk
equals positive action. The resultant action, negative or
positive, is the product of our inner programming. Therefore, controlling our inner voice is a matter of controlling
the course of our lives. There are no options in this matter
if we wish to live more positively, more productively.

Retraining the mind begins when we wake up in the
morning. When the negative messages start, we need to
recognize them and stop them. At that moment, we need
to tape over the negative messages. If I say to myself,
"You are not doing well today, Chris," I will not do well. I
will do well if I say, "You are a strong woman, Chris, and
you can handle anything that comes your way today." Or
even better, "This is going to be a great day today. God is
with me today. God is the love in which I live." The positive prompting nullifies the original negative message.

Then what? Keep it up. All day long? You bet! Whenever
your inner voice comes up with anything negative, counter
it. Otherwise with each negative jab, you will lose ground
and finally begin to believe the negative messages. It will
be a disastrous day because you have invited disaster into
your world. Little things that ordinarily bother you will be
devastating. Negative inner talk produces negative actions.

How long does this conscious effort to reprogram negative messages go on? Every few minutes if necessary.
With practice, the power of the negative messages dimin-
ishes and the positive track takes over.

To accomplish this important task of reprogramming our
inner voice, we need to be ready with a counter program,
one that will persistently and effectively override the old
messages of the past. Here are some steps to follow:

Step One: Listen In

The first step in our reversal comes when we listen carefully to our inner speech. Every minute of every day we are talking to ourselves from the inside out. When we hear negative messages like these we are in trouble: "I better watch out; bad things always happen to me. This is going to be another lousy day!" If I tell myself bad things, bad things will happen!

It is a matter of timing. What chance do I have when I am anticipating defeat, attack or danger? I throw my timing off by anticipating these calamities. I need to listen to my inner voice and hear clearly what I am saying. Are there any "shoulds"? Where did these "shoulds" come from? My childhood days, perhaps? From sibling rivalry or from overzealous parents? Locked away in my subconscious are negative messages that repeat themselves whenever triggered.

Recently, I found myself in a negative spin and couldn't figure out why. It seemed as if everything was happening at once and that I couldn't cope. As one problem arose, several others came up at the same time. I felt overwhelmed. Then I took some time to listen to my inner voice. For four months I had undergone stress. First came the death of a loved one, then several setbacks for those who are closest to me. Death had disoriented me and left me grieving, and personal disappointments had added abrupt changes that shook my confidence. I felt out of control.

When I listened, I heard doubt. My inner voice was saying so many things that related to performance:

Self-Doubt

1. I can't think straight.
2. I can't go on with this schedule. It's too exhausting.
3. Am I wasting my life doing what I am doing?

Relationships

Then it went into relationship issues:

1. I need to be with people. I am alone too much.
2. Am I concentrating too much on certain relationships?
3. Am I rejecting intimacy in relationships?
4. I need to do more to develop a primary relationship.

What-Ifs

Then it got into what-ifs:

1. What if I was still married? Where would I be today?
2. Did I make a mistake? Was I too hasty?
3. Why can't I find the right person to build my life with?

Feelings

Then it went to feelings:

1. I feel damaged and broken.
2. I am vulnerable now.

By listening to my negative self-talk, I realized that I had been courting this miserable state that I found myself in. In reality, my doubts about my performance were unfounded. As a matter of fact, they were refuted by some rather startling successes. By returning to the same old words in my thoughts, I was revisiting old doubts and fears.

In *Beyond Negative Thinking, Reclaiming Our Life Through Optimism*, Joseph T. Martorano and John P. Kildahl tell us:

> By focusing on your thinking, which is the cornerstone of your personality, you can achieve real personal growth. The one precept to keep in mind is: *You are what you think.* Remember also that you have the right and wherewithal to direct your thinking into channels that work for you. It's your mind!

By focusing on exactly what I was thinking, by putting it down on paper, by admitting that I really was thinking that way, I began to understand what was happening to me. I was programming my mind into that doubtful, negative state. Therefore I felt negative.

Once the list of my negative thoughts was made, I could see the pattern and make the necessary adjustments. It became very clear to me that I needed to override the negative thoughts with positive ones:

1. I am coping. I am a survivor.
2. I am working in a worthwhile profession and I am great at what I do.
3. I choose to enjoy my relationships.
4. I am making good decisions about intimate relationships.
5. I am working several self-help programs and I am sober 14 years today.
6. I am exactly where I should be today.
7. I am whole within myself, protected — a child of God.

With the awareness derived from listening to my inner voice, I began to combat the damaging negative messages of the past. Next I had to stop these messages and change my mental perspective.

Step Two: Stop The Message

After I realized what those negative messages were doing to me, I began aggressively to change my perspective. As soon as the damaging thought came to the forefront of my mind, I said, "*Stop*." No way would I entertain anything negative. It took concentration and diligence to rout those old messages. By stopping them as soon as they started, I was able to switch to a more positive mode.

Step Three: Switch To The Positive

As soon as I dismissed a damaging remark such as, "I can't go on with this pressure," I would immediately say to myself, "I am a survivor. One day at a time, Chris. I can do anything for only one day." Things began to ease. When I worried about being single and surviving alone, I would say, "Today, I am making good decisions about intimate relationships." Someplace inside I heard the new message and the tension eased. I did not feel so vulnerable, so alone. Just stopping the negative message was not enough, I needed to hear the positive messages in order to feel positive again. Each time I heard a negative message, I said, "*Stop*," and switched to the positive message. It began to work — positive things were happening again.

Step Four: Taking An Overview

As I began to get onto a positive track, it became easier to see the pattern of my life. I could look back at all the positive things that have happened to me and reassure myself that good things would happen again. I had become stuck in a negative maelstrom and the storm created hesitant, self-conscious negative behaviors. I needed to take an overview of my life and see the pattern of positives rather than get consumed in one negative spot.

When I am spinning out of control in a negative place, I am disoriented, unbalanced, afraid and confused. So it takes a clear, realistic look at my situation to make it right. Making a list helped because it was obviously lopsided toward the negative. Reason alone told me that something was wrong. A quick overview of my life showed that it wasn't "all bad." I challenged the reality of my negative thinking and came back to a more balanced view. Then I began to search for the reasons behind the negative thinking.

Performance negatives can hide procrastination problems. Interpersonal relationship questions can hide a genuine fear of rejection. Social problems can be related to recovery from addiction. Nothing is as it seems on the surface. Negative thinking can be a safe place. If you say you can't perform, you may not be asked to do so. If you don't search out intimacy, you can't be rejected. And if you are a failure, you don't have to deal with the added responsibility of success. There are certain payoffs to negative thinking.

Getting honest is not always easy. Taking an overview of where you are psychologically can be painful, as it can show that change is necessary. Sometimes it seems easier to stay on a negative track than find the courage to change the things we can.

Step Five: Using Self-Discipline

1. Break The Mental Ritual

Breaking the ritual of negative thinking is necessary if we are to live positive, productive lives. These rituals are so ingrained that we sometimes don't even notice them until we listen to ourselves and start switching our thinking.

For example, instead of berating myself for eating too much, I need to think slender by saying, "I am the right weight and I choose to eat what is good for me." Don't wait until you say, "I am fat." Use mental self-discipline to counter negative thinking.

2. Have A Plan

Begin the day by looking in the mirror and saying, "I love and approve of myself just as I am." Continue saying, "I approve of myself" throughout the day. Do it until it becomes engraved in your mind. Search for the good things about yourself, about your life. Note these things throughout the day. Silently comment on them.

3. Be Grateful

Thank God for the good things in your life. Since gratitude implies acceptance, it leads to inner peace.

Gratitude goes hand in hand with love, and where one is the other must be found.

For me, gratitude is a therapy that goes hand in hand with everyday living. In an attempt to capture this sense of everyday gratitude, I wrote down 33 times when we might be thankful:

A Litany Of Gratitude

I am thankful . . .

1. When it is below zero, and the car starts — and the heater works.
2. When the precipitation turns to rain, the storm goes out to sea and we are dry by the fire.
3. When there is hot oatmeal, milk and raisins on a winter morning.
4. When trains, trucks, airplanes and overnight express can deliver what we urgently need.
5. When we have the money to pay for the brand names on the supermarket shelves.
6. When we can see the bright colors of Christmas, the whiteness of snow and the permanence of the ocean.
7. When a rainbow emerges, the traffic light turns green and I am only a mile from home.
8. When a healthy child is born with ten tiny fingers and ten tiny toes.
9. When energetic toddlers finally settle down and go to sleep.
10. When your adult children phone you without being prompted.
11. When it is dark and someone turns on the light, or when it is too bright and someone dims the glare.
12. When a friend walks beside you, holds your hand, hears your words and responds gently.
13. When someone is willing to help rake the leaves or plant the garden.
14. When someone says, "I love you" or "You did a great job," "I'm sorry" or "Thank you."

15. When we hear God's voice in the voice of others —
    or from within.
16. When we can work at a job, negotiate a compro-
    mise, figure out the computer or pay the bills.
17. When there is silence without loneliness, noise with-
    out confusion.
18. When the furnace turns on with a comforting chug
    or the kitchen clock chimes cheerily on the wall.
    When we hear the civilized music of Bach after a
    stressed-out day at work.
19. When we hear the church bells toll, the school choir
    sing and the tugboat whistle.
20. When we come home and see the bike in the drive-
    way, toys on the floor and a wagging-tail dog to
    greet us.
21. When we realize how much we love our mothers,
    fathers, stepmothers, stepfathers, brothers, sisters,
    stepbrothers, stepsisters, grandparents, aunts and
    uncles — anyone we call family.
22. When we find something we had "lost" or experi-
    ence a fond memory.
23. When we laugh out loud, cry in our pillow or get
    angry — when we can feel our feelings.
24. When the operation is over, the pain is gone and we
    can move easily again.
25. When there's a time for mending and an opportu-
    nity to forgive.
26. When we enjoy the freedom to speak and pray and
    worship and vote.
27. When we come to accept a loss, by death or divorce
    — even when we don't understand why.
28. When we are peaceful inside.
29. When our shoes fit.
30. When we put on an old sweater, open a new book,
    find a chair in the sun — and read.

31. When the bubbles build in the bathtub, the towel is soft and we snuggle in bed.
32. When we think of the love of God, who makes all things work together for good.
33. When we experience the joys of life which are God's will for His children . . . We give thanks!

A Course In Miracles teaches us a great deal about the power of our minds. It says that "all thinking produces form at some level." The purpose of the *Course* is to retrain our minds in a systematic way to achieve a different perspective of everyone and everything in the world. The *Course* says every thought brings either peace or war; every thought either judges and therefore separates, or forgives and joins, bringing peace. We have no neutral thoughts and all thoughts have power!

If our thoughts carry such power, we need to discipline ourselves patiently to control them. Keep at it. Challenge yourself. Don't give up. When resistance takes hold, fight it. It won't be easy to erase old mental tapes but it will be worthwhile.

Retraining our minds is the work of spiritual recovery. When you falter, call on the Holy Spirit to guide you. Risk! Be willing to love yourself, to affirm yourself, to fight the negative thoughts of the past that wish to capture your power. Be willing to do whatever it takes to change the pattern of your thinking. Do exercises. Do mirror work. Pray! Meditate! Do positive visualizations of what you wish to happen. Be bold! Take a stand with your inner voice. Be good to yourself! You are a child of God.

Because everyone's spiritual journey is different, there is no set plan you must follow. Therefore, you need not adopt any specific formula. However, you need to decide on your plan, find what works for you and summon the mental discipline to execute that plan. Remember, it is a given that if you think positively, you will act positively.

How To Live In Love

I suggest you live in love. Here is how it works:

1. Living in love begins when we look within.
2. It starts with positive thoughts of self-love.
3. Trust develops and fear fades.
4. Others fear us less.
5. We experience expansiveness in all relationships.
6. We are kinder and more loving to others.
7. We generate love in all relationships by being more available to others.
8. We give positive feedback to others.
9. More positive messages come back to us.
10. A cycle of giving and receiving is set in motion in which life and love have new meaning.

A Course In Miracles reminds us:

> **Your task is not to seek for love, but merely to seek and find all the barriers within yourself that you have built against it.**

Your inner voice reflects your level of love because, as the *Course* says, "Love will enter immediately into any mind that truly wants it." Do you really want to change the way you speak to yourself? Do you want to speak to yourself in a loving voice? Do you really believe you are God's child, worthy of love itself? Do you really believe love, which created you, is what you are? If you do, then tell yourself this good news.

Giving And Receiving Are One

Sometimes we do not recognize what we receive until we give it away. Sometimes we need to hear ourselves speak the message so that we fully understand it ourselves. Real giving is not of material possessions but of forgiveness and love. We can be messengers of love! If I love myself as God's child, I will live a life of love — that is the only gift I need to give anyone.

The primary relationship in our lives is between ourselves and God. When that relationship is not nurtured, there is a spiritual void within. So it is to this primary connection we must be bound, and we must give it priority.

If we give ourselves to another human being in such an exclusive way that we forget our commitment to God, we will lose our way. Actually, we are saying to God, "I will attend to you after I attend to my lover. I make that human relationship my higher power. It dominates my mind; it controls my life. I am co-dependent and do not have time for you, God."

Spiritual intimacy with God transcends human relationships. Addiction and co-addiction involve the forgetting of God or, at best, putting another first or on an equal level with God. We nurture our relationship with God by making conscious contact with Him — we reach within. It means directing the mind to that loving place of comfort, by thinking and speaking to God. When we make conscious contact with God, His loving presence becomes evident in all things. There is possession of a living spirituality.

Prayer And Meditation

The first thing we must give to God is the acknowledgment that He is the primary force in our lives. We reach out through prayer, reading and meditation. In *Spirituality And Recovery*, Father Leo Booth says:

> Meditation is a technique of realizing our full potential as human beings and living our lives to the fullest. It is about finding time and discovering the time "to be." It is placing the physical, mental and emotional aspects of our lives in an at-one-ment. It is using silence to say yes.

There are no set patterns for meditation since it is primarily experiential. It is being still and knowing God. It is being still and being grateful to God. It is concentrating on peace or love until we internalize them. It may be reading special words meditatively. It may be different for each person but for all it awakens the spark of the Divine within us.

By paying too much attention to human relationships, career goals or even the care and management of a home, we can lose our spiritual center, fail to contact God and forget that He is our primary relationship. When that happens, we are looking for happiness in the material world of people and things. That never works. Real joy is inside us.

Contact with lovers, friends and family bring special joyous moments because we receive what we give. But first we need to give to God. We need to have our spirits charged. It takes energy to give of ourselves. When there is little energy inside, we are soon depleted.

When the ups and downs of life overwhelm me, I am powerless. Yet when I am in the right place with God, there is always enough power to accept and deal with the obstacles of life. God, the creator of all love, gives me enough love to live, to forgive, to accept and to grow. My first step must be to give of myself in this primary relationship with God. Then when I receive His Love, I will be ready to go on with my life.

How To Be A Messenger Of God

Once we have given ourselves to this love relationship with God, the next thing we must do is to share that love with others. We cannot keep to ourselves what we receive from God. In order to keep it, we must give it away. In this sense, we become the messengers of God's love, of His word.

The Course taught me:

A messenger is not one who writes the message he delivers. Nor does he question the right of Him who does, or ask why he has chosen the message he brings.

When we are in a close relationship with God, we become His messengers. We perform our part by first accepting His message of love for ourselves, then we show we understand it by giving it away. We choose no roles that are not given by Him and we gain by every message of love we give away.

The concept that "giving and receiving are one" is new to me. But it is true. Whenever I do something that is loving, whenever I extend light or energy in a positive way, it comes back to me. There are no exceptions to these mini-miracles: They just keep happening.

No one can receive and understand he has received until he gives. For in the giving is his own acceptance of what he has received.

But what are we specifically asked to give? At first that was a mystery to me because I was thinking in terms of material possessions. Does it mean we give all our goods to those less fortunate?

In most instances, giving has little to do with the material world. Real giving means forgiveness and love. If I love myself, as God's child, I will live a life of love. That is the only gift I ever need to give anyone.

When I came to understand that all situations were teaching/learning situations, I began to see that giving and receiving are one. The lines of separateness that I draw between myself and others fade and disappear.

The world recedes as we light up our minds, as we make God our primary focus, as we assimilate his message of love into our being and carry that message to others. We do not recognize the message we have heard until we give it to others. Then we can receive it for ourselves.

You will not see the light until you offer it to all your brothers. As they take it from your hands, so will you recognize it as your own.

How To Discern God's Message

Once we have established a primary relationship with our Creator and accepted our place in the universe as His children, we are ready for our life's work. We turn our will and our life over to the care of God as we understand Him. As God's children, we already have all we need. We are complete in our own oneness with God. Therefore, it matters little what we do for a living. How we execute our chosen career does matter.

We are here to project God's message of love, not to operate a tractor-trailer truck, write a legal document, pave a road, cure a patient or lecture to an audience. We are of love itself, of God, and our purpose is to love. We can bless the world when we use the surgeon's knife, teach someone the alphabet, serve someone a bowl of soup or scrub the floor. We can love wherever we are.

All of us are messengers — we will project some message whether it be God's message of love or messages of fear, resentment and hatred. We will cry out for love or we will give love, either way bringing a message to the world.

Having choices allows us to teach love or fear. By turning our life and will over to the care of God as we understand Him, we are making the decision to go with God's purpose, and God's purpose can only be a loving one.

It is not always necessary that we understand the direction of our lives, but it is essential that we understand the purpose. Our purpose can only be to bless the world in God's love. We are God's children and we are truly on our father's business. But how do we do this?

First, we need to see everyone as ONE — equal, special, unique — all God's children. This realization removes pride, prejudice and judgment. Spiritually, there are no differences in us. Our purpose is to reach out in love to all who touch our lives. It doesn't have to be the sick and suffering children in Africa. It can be the weary senior citizen who bags the groceries at the supermarket. We can help him out by putting a few of the groceries into the bag, smiling and saying thank you. Let him know you love and appreciate his work.

Second, we need to be grateful for every moment of our lives because every moment provides us an opportunity to be a channel of God's love. All we need to do is recognize the opportunities for love that are ours.

Living in the moment can mean giving a child who stutters time to speak, listening to a friend's concerns about her husband's health, being grateful to know that child or that friend. Through our loving attention, we can give others the gift of love. Even when we are in emotional pain, we can be grateful for the opportunity to feel our feelings and to grow to a new place of emotional strength. Even when we have been betrayed, we can be grateful for the opportunity to grow through forgiveness.

Through our loving words, we can contribute to a positive inner voice within others. We can bring to their subconscious messages that may return to them when they have lost confidence or are afraid. Words of love are powerful tools that shape future positive actions.

Once I refused to speak to someone who loved me. We had come to the point of ending our relationship and I had asked him not to contact me again, but it was Christmas Eve and he called. Out of fear I refused to enter into the conversation. I said I did not want to speak with him at this time. I was forceful, adamant, explicit. Ten days later, he died in his sleep and I was denied the opportunity to ever speak to him again. At the gravesite, all I could do was put one red rose upon his cremated body.

That scene will never leave my mind. It is a bleak and horrible reminder of the transiency of life. Since that life-changing day, I try to speak what I feel and respect and honor all loving acts of others.

Last week it struck me that I owe a great debt to my daughter. She has always been emotionally available to me, patient and loving. We have an unusual relationship. Then I realized how necessary it was that I speak those words to her. Just because something "is" does not mean that it is "always recognized." I couldn't wait until the proper time to tell her what she means to me. It was a simple thing — we were together at a local restaurant having breakfast on a Saturday morning, as we have done so many times. I said, "I want you to know how much I love you and value our relationship. I am blessed to have you in my life." She has since told me that she has thought of that moment many times.

Through acceptance of my role as a child of God, I can bring peace to others. It is emotionally destructive to seek anything but peace of mind. Therefore, peace is my goal. Living in the moment means asking myself in all situations, "What is the loving thing to do here? How can I restore peace to this scene? What is my part in this? How can I be a channel of God's love here?" When I find my inner answers to these questions, I will be living in love.

Third, we can use the gifts God has given us to produce love in the world. It doesn't matter what our gifts may be, all gifts are of God.

It was as a writer that I first began to see my gifts "spring into my sight and leap into my hands." For a brief moment, I tried to claim these gifts because my ego told me they were mine. I began to plan trying to control my success. Almost immediately I recognized the fallacy in that thinking. I decided to write what was in my heart and leave any worldly success to God. That took my ego out of the picture and let me speak directly to the reader.

A Course In Miracles reminded me to let go of what I claimed as mine. Now I use my gifts to speak of God's love, but I do not claim these gifts. The Holy Spirit leads the way in my writing, and I follow. There is little difficulty with decision making in my choice of subject as I am led from one awareness to another. The goal is to speak of what I learn, to give it away to others — in love. There is no other goal.

In *A Return To Love*, Marianne Williamson says:

> We make decisions by asking the Holy Spirit to decide for us. There are always so many factors in life that we can't know. We make no decisions by ourselves, but ask how we might be most helpful in carrying out His plan. The moral authority that this attribute gives creates a starlike quality. It is our humility, our desire to be of service, that makes us stars. Not our arrogance.

As I write with this purpose in mind, I find myself energized by the process. It is not a difficult, arduous task that drains me of all my energy. It is a process that brings me energy, helping me to hear my own lessons, letting me learn as I teach, allowing me to receive as I give.

Giving and receiving have become one in my writing. As I expend the energy to reach out to you, new energy comes forth, revitalizing me. I never tire of the task for it has long ago ceased to be anything but a labor of love.

So it should be in the use of any God-given gift, whether creative or commercial. It really doesn't matter what I do but it matters very much why I do it. I have to ask myself: "Am I teaching love in what I do? Am I living as God's child each day?" All of us can heed these words in the *Course*:

> *Any situation must be to you a chance to teach others what they are, and what they are to you. No more than that, but also never less.*

Teaching God's love is not only the work of writers, artists, priests and missionaries, it is the work of the corporate president, the waiter, the janitor, the lawyer and the unemployed. It doesn't matter what you do, it only matters how you live. There is no other choice except to live in love if we are to be true to our spiritual selves. We do it by seeing all people as *one*, by gratefully living in the moment and by using our own unique gifts to bless the world.

So far in this chapter I have only spoken of giving, not of receiving. The reason is that giving and receiving are one. Whatever you give in love, in peace and in healing will be yours.

But still you might ask, "What do I receive?" The same things that you give! It is such a simple truth that sometimes the power of it eludes us.

> *You understand that you are healed when you give healing.*

By living in love what do you receive? The greatest gift of all. Peace! The *Course* says: "Peace comes to those who choose to heal and not to judge." Whenever we make a conscious choice to forgive, to heal a situation, we are giving the gift of peace to ourselves as well as the other person. It is like a circle where the peace you give comes right back to you. Could there be a better gift?

The *Course* maintains we are the essential instruments of peace for the world and that our thoughts and actions determine how widely it is shared. We become the means of peace when we are willing to learn, to teach, to give and especially to forgive.

There is an enormous difference between an unforgiving thought and forgiveness. An unforgiving thought is frantic in its intent, twisting relentlessly to pursue its goal. It holds distortion as its purpose and in a furious attempt, it tries to smash the reality of anything that gets in its way — any contradictory point of view.

Forgiveness, on the other hand, is still and quietly does nothing, nor seeks to twist it to appearances it likes. It merely looks, waits and judges not.

It seems ironic that by exerting no effort to judge, we can come to a peaceful place. It seems strange that by expecting nothing, we can gain it all. If I must be right or better or anything more than you, I will not be at peace.

Peace of mind brings happiness to me. Peace of mind brings me spiritual joy. It brings me to a oneness with myself and a oneness with you. There is no reason to be right or wrong, or more or less — that's not necessary with God's children.

What seems unfair sometimes causes me to lose my peace. But it is not my job to judge the fairness of life, to interpret the vagaries of the material world. It is my job to accept joyfully my true nature as a spiritual being, a child of God. Only then can I see you in the same light; only then will you respond to me in peace and love.

It is the function of love to unite not divide — to hold all things together. When we are loving, we attract love to us. We live in love.

It is as if the light of God's love within us draws the love of others to us. We become the messengers for God's love. In whatever we do, we teach love. We forgive. We heal. And ultimately it all comes back to us, bringing us healing, love and peace. The circle is complete through God, through love itself.

A Place Of Joy, Peace And Glory

10

Acceptance of the will of God brings joy and peace to us. The glory of God surrounds us even when we are blinded by resistance. As children of God, we are perfect. That is the mystery of life, the divine paradox, that we must accept. Living in love is living by our true nature — anything less leaves us restless. God's will for us is joy. Peace comes from removing guilt and resentment. Finally through humility we find glory.

All of us want to live joyfully, content with the world around us, without petty complaints, happy within — these are our goals. We can see joy in others, but how do we get it?

First, we need to recognize that God's will for us is joy. It is inconceivable that a loving parent could want anything but joy for his or her children. So it must be with God. Some people believe in a punishing God, who hands down judgments to teach us lessons. That is not my conception of God. For me, God is love itself and I am His child. The unhappiness we experience comes from an arbitrary material world.

So much of what we see in our everyday living is from the wrong perspective, our human perspective. We see material loss, violence, death and suffering. Trying to understand worldly suffering can become overwhelming. Perhaps we were never meant to understand it but to see it as a by-product of the material world. Perhaps, as it says in the *Course,* our human world is full of illusions, while the real world is spiritual, of God, of love itself. Perhaps the only permanent world is within our spiritual selves — the part of us that makes us children of God. I can readily accept that. It is so much simpler for me to accept God's will for me as joy and to leave the rest of the mysteries of the universe to the world of illusions.

I do not know why life includes so many tragic shifts and changes. I have failed in trying to make sense of it. But in some strange way, the world seems to work in conjunction with me when I cooperate with it.

By recognizing my primary relationship with God, I can let go of the things of this world and not expect to understand them. With God's help, I can let go of an addiction or an addictive relationship — knowing these things were not meant to bring me joy. Loss always includes some sadness, but the sadness is easier to bear when I do not resist the change, when I let go and let God.

As long as I played God, trying to control the world, I did not find happiness. When I let go and brought my will in line with God's, I found joy.

There are many times when we all need to say, "God is very good to me." Just look around and find the things you can be joyful about. Look to yourself. Are you in physical pain today? Celebrate. Are you able to see the rain on the window? Celebrate. If you can't see it, can you hear it? Again, celebrate. Have you been fed today? Celebrate. Can you tell somone you love them? Do it.

Joy is not found in the accumulation of wealth. It is found in the acceptance of God's goodness to us, in a benevolent universe and in our connection with love itself.

From an ego-based thought system, we see ourselves as separate from the world. Our material possessions don't matter. Nor does it matter who loves us. We think we can be more if we have more or can claim some identity from someone else. With this kind of thinking we are doomed to lose. Eventually the Mercedes will wear out, the house will rot and deteriorate and the one who loves us will die. The world teaches us to prepare to lose. Instead we need to prepare to return to God, to love itself.

What do I prize? What possesses me? Why? Usually we don't understand how tied we are to the things of the world until we lose them. When our health is good, we abuse it. We tend to take friends for granted. We think financial security will last forever. Not until we lose any of these things do we realize how much we depended on them.

In special relationships we often try to possess our lovers, and then, when we lose them, we grieve the loss. Each time we are brought back to humility and closer to our true spiritual selves. Ask any discerning individual who has suffered any worldly loss and they will admit a lesson was learned. It is through humility that we come to find God's glory.

A Course In Miracles speaks of "illusions." When we think we have lost something of this world, we are only losing the material which is transitory. The only permanent reality comes from God.

> *As you created me, I can give up nothing you gave me. What you did not give has no reality.*

We can continue to accumulate worldy possessions and try to gain happiness through illusions, but real happiness comes through peace of mind.

Although the mind's natural state is one of peace, for most of us peace is elusive. Many people believe that driving a luxury car, living by the ocean and having a home decorated with beautiful furnishings will bring happiness. We work to acquire more of the world, only to find that it does not bring us peace or contentment.

Peace can come by training our minds to correct all ego-based distortions.

> *Our peace of mind begins within with our own thoughts. It is from that peace of mind that a peaceful perspective of the world comes forth.*

Overcoming Obstacles To Serenity

There are many obstacles to peace of mind, but some are more obvious than others. Fear, guilt, anger and judgment are the primary foes.

Fear

Fear comes in many packages but basically it is a lack of faith. Although I know I am protected as God's child, it is easy to forget that and sink into fear-centered thinking. There are times when I fear not being accepted, when I fear success or failure or financial insecurity. Whenever I become mired in fear, I have lost contact with God. I have simply forgotten I am His child and He has the power to protect and heal me. It's ludricrous to believe that God would not take care of His own. Having faith in God is essential to inner peace.

Guilt

Guilt provides another obstacle to serenity. To see ourselves as flawed and sinful is to lose sight of our basic spiritual nature. Guilt is self-imposed punishment inflicted for violating our self-imposed standards. Guilt over our unloving acts can produce healthy remorse and change, but we need not continue to attack ourselves, refusing to forgive ourselves. Our negative behavior has not changed our basic spiritual nature. We are still no less than children of God. We are one with God.

Guilt keeps us stuck in the past and afraid of the future, thinking we are yet to be punished. Anyone afflicted with guilt has lost sight of the unchanging and eternal. Guilt keeps us locked into our ego-based thinking.

On the other hand, a feeling of guiltlessness makes it possible to forgive ourselves and others. When I feel forgiven, I can grant that same forgiveness to someone else.

Check your thinking. Are you thinking of others as guilty while you see yourself as innocent? In order to stay in a peaceful state of mind, it is necessary to not ascribe guilt, either to yourself or others.

Are you thinking of yourself as guilty? Check to see if you really believe you are God's child. Check to see if you are thinking that you can be perfect, rather than that you are a perfect child of God.

Feeling less than perfect isolates us from peace, love and joy. When we fail to be all that we can be, as we inevitably do, we often feel guilty. Some of us are tormented by the things we "should do" or "should not do." Living becomes a panorama of decisions. What must we do to be right or avoid being wrong? How can we possibly be perfect?

The truth is we are already perfect, even in our humanness. We are made in the image and likeness of God, of love itself. It does no good to chase perfection. It does no good to say, "I will be happy when I become a perfect mother, father, brother, sister or lover." We are all as perfect as we can be at this moment. We have already been forgiven our imperfections.

Fear and guilt are twin emotions that feed on each other. Whenever there is guilt, there is implied punishment. The thought of punishment engenders fear. Fearful persons cannot be fully alive because they are trying to earn their perfection, trying to protect themselves.

As long as we live in love, and teach love rather than fear, we need not feel guilty. If we can see that forgiveness is our primary function, we are more likely to see ourselves as perfect children of God.

As Joan Borysenko says in *Guilt Is The Teacher, Love Is The Answer*,

> Many of us lose touch with our indwelling Divine nature — the unlimited creative potential of love that Jesus assured us could literally move mountains.

When we live in fear, we live without faith.

Unless we see ourselves as sinless through forgiveness, we will always be trying to make up for our imperfections. Unless we see others also as sinless, we will condemn and judge, refusing to forgive them.

Condemnation of others obstructs peace of mind. When we judge and blame, we give up our own happiness.

Peace of mind is our joy — it is the ultimate joy! Yet many times we disturb our peaceful state by making judgements, by determining who is right and who is wrong. It doesn't matter.

*In quietness are all things answered, and is every
problem quietly resolved.*

In *Goodbye To Guilt*, Gerald Jampolsky says relationships
can be healed by "saying goodbye to guilt" and letting go
of the fear that separates us. He says:

> We release guilt from the past through forgiveness.
> Ironically if we go through the process of forgiving others,
> we will come to forgive ourselves.

Fears encourage guilt; when we no longer find it necessary to ascribe guilt to someone else, we can accept love.
It is through love that we find our freedom. Whenever we
give too much attention to what we own, or who we
relate to, or how our children act, or what we do for a
living, we can lose our happiness and peace of mind. Fear,
guilt and condemnation are obstacles to peace. When we
return to love, to our true selves, we find joy, peace and
glory waiting for us.

The *Course* suggests that we suffer from a case of mis-
taken identity. We have forgotten our true self, which is
said to be limitless, transcendent and eternal. Instead we
regard ourselves as a separate self, limited to the body.
Feeling fearful and defenseless, we look to the fleeting
pleasures of this world as our only source of satisfaction.

As I said before, we find the glory of God through the
humble realization that we are "children" — God's children. It often takes a severe loss to reach that moment of
humility, that "spiritual awakening." For some, it is the
moment they realize they are addicted. For some, it is the
moment a loved one turns away. Some reach bottom when
they lose their role in life, when they can no longer say
they are respected at work or at home.

We all eventually hit a low point, a bottom, where all
seems lost. The glory we anticipated from the material
world is suddenly gone. Our job is lost. Our wife has left.

Our child is dead. Our friend has turned against us. Our parents are no longer there. Where do we go then?

In a brief, tragic moment, we come to understand there is no permanent glory in the things of this world. If we only look to them for our fulfillment, we will eventually lose. But when that happens, we could be forced to look to God to seek His assistance.

In the most paradoxical way, we awaken spiritually to the truth that we cannot become permanently attached to anyone. Yet we must be attached in love to everyone. We learn that the only connection is the one we already have — to God, to love itself. We learn that we have been looking for our peace, joy, freedom and glory in the wrong places. It will never come from that which is outside of us. But it will come when we go inside, to love itself, to our spiritual selves. By humbly asking God for help, we recognize our true divine estate, our humble, yet glorious, position as a child of God. Here we find our glory.

Joy, peace and glory are not experienced yesterday or tomorrow; they are ours today. They are ours at this moment — all we have to do is reach for them in love. Joy, peace and glory can't be denied us; they are a part of our spiritual self. To have them, all we need to do is return to love itself. God is with us this day. And every day.

Inspirations
To Open Your Heart

11

I offer you this list of reminders that I use as my litany when I forget how to live in love. May they bring you help along the way.

- *God made me just like Himself
  and God is love itself.*

- *I picture myself as a child of
  God with a new perspective, seeing all
  people as His children.*

- *I am confident, remembering God does
  not make rejects. I am precious.
  I am of love itself.*

*• I live like God's child. Letting
resentment, hatred and defenses go,
forgiving myself and others.*

*• I think like God's child,
accepting no abuse, misuse or ridicule.
I am lovable.*

*• I ask God's help.
I call home to talk to Him.*

*• I let the power of God touch
and direct my life. I become
spiritualized by God's love.*

- *I see love in all things:*
In the sun that shines on me,
in the rain that moistens the earth,
in the trees that bear fruit,
in the ocean and the wind.

- *I take strength from nature,*
allowing myself to be like the
sun, rain, ocean and wind.
I am just as I am.

- *I am not afraid.*
God's love drives out fear.
Love and fear cannot exist
in the same place.

- *I let love chase away the fear*
in others. I teach only love.

• *I allow love to heal all wounds.*
I forgive all others because
they are God's children too.
God has already forgiven all of us.

• *I turn over the difficult situations*
in my life to God.
He can handle them!

• *By prayer and meditation, I remember*
to focus on my relationship with God.

• *I won't return to the past.*
Nothing loving is happening there.

- *I won't allow fear to drag me
  into the future. Love hasn't
  happened there yet.*

- *I won't think of myself as a victim.
  I am full of the love, power
  and glory of God.*

- *I will give away love and it will
  return to me. Love is the only
  gift I need give anyone. Giving and
  receiving are one.*

- *I will associate with spiritual
  partners. People who wish to
  co-create love with me.*

- *I will listen to what you say.
  There is great meaning in words.
  I will speak lovingly.*

- *I will not question my message.*
  It is already written in the
  mind and heart of God.

- *I will speak lovingly to myself.*
  I will not criticize, berate or
  scare myself. I will be gentle
  with myself.

- *I will think positively about myself.*
  I will send loving messages to others.
  I will transmit love.

• *I will think positively about others,*
dismissing attacking thoughts because
they destroy love.

• *I will put everything in a loving space.*
Changing from the inside out, I will
enjoy a new loving me.

• *Finding power in defenselessness,*
I will walk away from always being right.
I am God's child. I am perfect as I am.

• *I am grateful for my life.*
I see God's gifts around me.

• *I accept that God will not bring me*
harm and that all things work together
for good. I will accept God's will
in all things.

• *I know God's will for me is joy.*
I am his precious child.

• *I realize God's glory surrounds me,*
even when I can't see it. I will
allow light in my life.

• *I am open to "holy instants."*
These coincidences are the
miracles of life.

• *I feel the peace of God in my heart.*
I will not let guilt, fear or resentment
steal away my peace of mind.
I will treasure it.

- *I can change the world for the better.*
  I can perfect it by living in love.

- *I can find comfort by knowing:*
  "God is the love in which I forgive."
  "God is the love in which I live."

- *Through me, God's love shines on others.*
  And through you, God's love shines on me.

Endnotes

Chapter One:

3. Nathaniel Branden, **How To Raise Your Self-Esteem,** (New York, NY: Bantam Books, 1987.) p. 5-9.

5. **A Course In Miracles,** (Tiburon, CA: Foundation For Inner Peace, 1975.) Text p. 100.

13. Louise L. Hay, **The Power Is Within You,** (Santa Monica, CA: Hay House, Inc., 1991.) p. 95.

16. **A Course In Miracles,** Workbook, p. 65.

Chapter Two:

21. Gerald G. Jampolsky, M.D., **Out Of The Darkness Into The Light,** (New York, NY: Bantam Books, 1989.) p. 11.

22. Hugh Prather, **This Is The Place Where You Are Not Alone — Reflections On A Course In Miracles,** (New York, NY: Doubleday, 1980.) p. 25.

22. Marianne Williamson, **A Return To Love — Reflections and Principles of A Course In Miracles,** (New York, NY: Harper Collins Publishers, 1992.) p. 49.

24. Marianne Williamson, p. 54.

24. **A Course In Miracles,** Workbook, p. 107.

28. **Twelve Steps and Traditions,** (New York, NY: Alcoholics Anonymous World Services, Inc., 1953.) p. 8.

30. **A Course In Miracles,** Workbook p. 392, Workbook p. 392, Workbook, p. 412, Workbook, p. 430.

31. **A Course In Miracles,** Workbook, p. 430.

Chapter Three:

37. **A Course In Miracles,** Workbook p. 73.

40. Gerald G. Jampolsky, M.D., **Love Is Letting Go Of Fear** (Berkley, CA: Celestial Arts, 1979.) p. 24.

41. **A Course In Miracles,** Workbook, p. 437.

46. **A Course In Miracles,** Workbook, p. 213.

47. **A Course In Miracles,** Workbook, p. 404.

Chapter Four:

51. Marianne Williamson, p. 27.

51. **A Course In Miracles,** Workbook, p. 396.

52. **A Course In Miracles,** Workbook, p. 396.

54. Marianne Williamson, p. 12.

55. Ken Keyes, Jr. and Bruce Burkan, **How To Make Your Life Work Or Why Aren't You Happy?** (Coos Bay, OR: Living Love Publications, 1974).

58. Lewis M. Andrews, **To Thine Own Self Be True** (New York, NY: Doubleday, 1987.) p. 23-49.

59. **A Course In Miracles,** Workbook, p. 155.

Chapter Five:

65. **A Course In Miracles,** Workbook, p. 71.

65. Marianne Williamson, p. 16.

68. **A Course In Miracles,** Workbook, p. 419.

69. Gerald G. Jampolsky, **Teach Only Love** (New York, NY: Bantam Books, 1983.) p. 41.

Chapter Six:

74. Lee Jampolsky, **Healing The Addictive Mind** (Berkley CA: Celestial Arts, 1991.)

75. **A Course In Miracles,** Text, p. 132.

78. Lee Jampolsky, p. 30.

78. **A Course In Miracles,** Workbook, p. 83.

80. Gay Hendricks and Kathlyn Hendricks, **Conscious Loving** (New York, NY: Bantam Books, 1990.) p. 84.

82. Gay Hendricks and Kathlyn Hendricks, p. 105.

87. **A Course In Miracles,** Text, p. 435.

Chapter Seven:

95. Frances Vaughn and Roger Walsh, **Accept This Gift** (New York, NY: Putnam Publishing Group, 1983.) Foreword.

95. Tara Singh, **A Course In Miracles — A Gift For All Mankind** (Los Angeles, CA: Life Action Press, 1992.) p. 9.

96. **A Course In Miracles,** Workbook, p. 71.

97. **A Course In Miracles,** Introduction.

97. **A Course In Miracles,** Text, p. 84.

98. **A Course In Miracles,** Text, p. 92.

99. **A Course In Miracles,** Workbook, p. 189.

99. **A Course In Miracles,** Workbook, p. 277.

Chapter Eight:

114. Joseph T. Martorano and John P. Kildahl, **Beyond Negative Thinking** (New York, NY: Avon Books, 1989.) p. 22.

117. **A Course In Miracles,** Workbook, p. 363.

120. **A Course In Miracles,** Text, p. 27.

121. **A Course In Miracles,** Text, p. 315.

Chapter Nine:

125. Father Leo Booth, **Spirituality and Recovery** (Deer-

field Beach, FL: Health Communications, Inc., 1985.) p. 84.

127. **A Course In Miracles,** Workbook, p. 154.

127. **A Course In Miracles,** Workbook, p. 154.

128. **A Course In Miracles,** Workbook, p. 278.

130. **A Course In Miracles,** Workbook, p. 283.

131. Marianne Williamson, p. 176-177.

132. **A Course In Miracles,** MT I.

132. **A Course In Miracles,** Workbook, p. 293.

133. **A Course In Miracles,** Workbook, p. 391.

Chapter Ten:

139. **A Course In Miracles,** Workbook, p. 452.

139. **A Course In Miracles,** Workbook, p. 51.

141. Joan Borysenko, Ph.D. **Guilt Is The Teacher — Love Is The Lesson** (New York, NY: Warner Books, 1990.) p. 23.

142. Gerald G. Jampolsky, M.D. **Goodbye To Guilt** (New York, NY: Bantam Books, 1985.) Introduction.

Reading List

Andrews, Lewis M. **To Thine Own Self Be True.** Doubleday, New York, NY: 1987.

Booth, Father Leo. **Spirituality And Recovery.** Health Communications, Inc., Deerfield Beach, FL: 1985.

Branden, Nathaniel. **How To Raise Your Self-Esteem.** Bantam Books, New York, NY: 1987.

Hay, Louise L. **The Power Is Within You.** Hay House, Inc., Santa Monica, CA: 1991.

Hendricks, Gay and Kathlyn Hendricks. **Conscious Loving.** Bantam Books, New York, NY: 1990.

H.T.P. **Turning It Over: How To Find Tranquility When You Never Thought You Could.** Health Communications, Inc., Deerfield Beach, FL: 1992.

Jampolsky, Gerald G., M.D. **Goodbye To Guilt.** Bantam Books, New York, NY: 1985.

Jampolsky, Gerald G., M.D. **Love Is Letting Go Of Fear.** Celestial Arts, Berkeley, CA: 1979.

Jampolsky, Gerald G., M.D. **Out Of The Darkness Into The Light.** Bantam Books, New York, NY: 1989.

Jampolsky, Gerald G., M.D. and Diane Cirincione. **Love Is The Answer: Creating Positive Relationships.** Bantam Books, New York, NY: 1990.

Jampolsky, Lee. **Healing The Addictive Mind.** Celestial Arts, Berkeley, CA: 1991.

Keyes, Ken, Jr. and Bruce Burkan. **How To Make Your Life Work Or Why Aren't You Happy?** Living Love Publications, Coos Bay, OR: 1974.

McKenna, Christine A. **Love, Infidelity And Sexual Addiction, A Co-dependent's Perspective.** Abbey Press, St. Meinrad, MN: 1992.

Martorano, Joseph T. and John P. Kildahl. **Beyond Negative Thinking.** Avon Books, New York, NY: 1989.

Peck, M. Scott, M.D. **The Road Less Traveled.** Simon and Schuster, New York, NY: 1978.

Prather, Hugh. **This Is A Place Where You Are Not Alone — Reflections On A Course In Miracles.** Doubleday, New York, NY: 1980.

Simon, Sidney, Dr. and Suzanne Simon. **Forgiveness — How To Make Peace With Your Past And Get On With Your Life.** Warner Books, New York, NY: 1990.

Singh, Tara. **A Course In Miracles: A Gift For All Mankind.** Life Action Press, Los Angeles, CA: 1986.

Singh, Tara. **Love Holds No Grievances.** Foundation For Life Action, Los Angeles, CA: 1986.

Stairway To Serenity: The Eleventh Step. Hazelden Foundation, Center City, MN: 1988.

The Song Of Prayer: Prayer, Forgiveness, Healing. Foundation For Inner Peace, Tiburon, CA: 1978.

Twelve Steps And Traditions. Alcoholics Anonymous World Services, Inc., New York, NY: 1953.

Vaughn, Frances and Roger Walsh. **Accept This Gift.** Putnam Publishing Group, New York, NY: 1983.

Vaughn, Frances and Roger Walsh. **A Gift Of Peace: Selections From A Course In Miracles.** Putnam Publishing Group, New York, NY: 1986.

Williamson, Marianne. **A Return To Love: Reflections And Principles Of A Course In Miracles.** Harper Collins Publishers, New York, NY: 1992.

Make a difference in your life with

THE MAGAZINE FOR PERSONAL GROWTH

Changes

CHANGES is the only national magazine that keeps you informed about the latest and best in personal growth and recovery. It's filled with personal "how to" advice for developing positive growth and happiness in all areas of your life.

Friendly, understanding and down-to-earth, CHANGES offers thought-provoking feature stories and exciting special sections. Plus — every issue brings you "Living Better" — six enlightening features aimed at helping you heal and strengthen the important aspects of your life: Feelings, Relationships, Body, Working, Self-Esteem and Spirit.

Order CHANGES today and see why thousands of others consider it to be an integral part of their positive growth plan. Our special offer to you: One year of CHANGES (six bi-monthly issues) for just $16.95. That's 44% off the regular subscription price, and a fraction of the annual newsstand price.

Clip and mail this coupon to:
Changes Magazine, P.O. Box 609, Mount Morris, IL 61054-0609

Yes!

Enter my subscription ( ) one year for $16.95*
to CHANGES for: ( ) two years for $34.00

Name: _____

Address: _____

City: _____ State: _____ Zip: _____

☐ Payment enclosed ☐ Please bill me   QCA93
Charge my ☐ VISA ☐ MC #: _____

Exp. _____ Signature: _____

*Basic price: $30/yr. FL residents add 6% state sales tax. Canadian and foreign rate: $23.50 per year with order, US funds. GST included.